PLANNING IN EAST EUROPE

Industrial Management
by the State

Planning
in East Europe

*Industrial Management
by the State*

A BACKGROUND BOOK

Michael Kaser

*Lecturer in Soviet Economics, University of Oxford
Fellow of St. Antony's College, Oxford*

Janusz G. Zieliński

*Docent and Head of the Research Unit for Price and
Incentive Theory, Central School of Planning
and Statistics, Warsaw*

THE BODLEY HEAD
LONDON   SYDNEY
TORONTO

© Michael Kaser and
Janusz Zieliński 1970
ISBN 0 370 00397 7
Printed and bound in Great Britain for
The Bodley Head Ltd
9 Bow Street, London, WC2
by William Clowes & Sons Ltd, Beccles
Set in Linotype Plantin
First published 1970

CONTENTS

ACKNOWLEDGMENTS

RESEARCH ON contemporary east European economics at St Antony's College, Oxford, has received financial support from the Social Science Research Council, the Joseph Retinger Memorial Fund (administered by the Institute for International Education), and the Leverhulme Trust: the authors gratefully acknowledge assistance from these sources.

The coverage of the current year's developments in Czechoslovakia was much facilitated by the presence in the College of Mr L. Rychetník, on leave from the Charles University, Prague; Mr I. Şpigler was of help on documentation; and Dr R. Portes kindly made general comments.

December, 1969

I
Politics of Control

THE MANAGEMENT of industry in eastern Europe patently differs from that in western Europe in the nationalisation of the individual enterprise and the central planning of the entire economy. While the change took place as a consequence of political revolution after the Second World War, and in emulation of the Soviet system, east European industry even before the war had tended to be more subject to government intervention than elsewhere on the Continent.

The succession to empires—Tsarist, Austrian, Prussian and Ottoman—of small independent kingdoms and republics after the First World War broke up the markets towards which early east European industrialisation had been directed; the Great Depression—and, for east Europe particularly, far-reaching bank failures—drove private enterprise further to-wards tariff protection and government support. Economic nationalism, concomitant with state intervention, was a mild prelude to postwar expropriation and rigid direction, but in-dicates how political factors have perennially influenced the course of east European economic management.

Once communist parties were established as governments, aligning their foreign policy to that of the USSR, the form of that management was subject to national and international factors within the communist movement. The major events to which changes in industrial control may be traced are the expulsion of Yugoslavia from the Cominform (1948), the death of Stalin in 1953, uprisings in Poland and Hungary during 1956, the Sino-Soviet dispute, which came into the open in 1960, and the 1968 occupation of Czechoslovakia. From the first emerged workers' self-government, whereby a director responsible to an elected council managed the opera-tions of the plant in the collective interest of those employed; the framework in which decisions were made was initially that

9

of a government plan, but subsequently that of a market. In Poland and Hungary workers' councils were a spearhead of revolt in 1956, but did not outlive the political circumstances that gave them birth. Nevertheless, like the continuing example of Yugoslavia, their brief existence has underscored a socialist alternative to Stalin's planning: it is profit-orientated in practice, but syndicalist, not capitalist, in ideology. Market syndicalism was one of the models on which a new Czechoslovak economic system was being put together during 1968; Bulgaria and Rumania also established worker-participation in their contemporaneous reforms, the one with, the other without, movement towards use of a market mechanism. In 1968, furthermore, Albania, which had steadfastly preserved the directive system it took from the USSR in 1956, launched a programme of 'workers' control'.

The lull in the Cold War during the three years from Stalin's death to the revolutions of Warsaw and Budapest moderated a little Soviet pressure on east Europe. Some of the excessive centralism was pruned from economic management, the USSR reduced its claim on domestic resources (exercised under the Peace Treaties through reparations and mixed companies), rationing was relaxed and production plans were revised to allow more satisfaction to the consumer.

In the wake of the 1956 upheavals Poland introduced a reform of the directive system which became the model for present industrial practice in the German Democratic Republic (GDR) and Rumania; Hungary initiated a decentralisation, the failure of which eventually convinced it of the need to break with directives in favour of a market. Two years later Czechoslovakia launched an attempt to combine enterprise initiative with central directives, the collapse of which, too, later shaped the market-orientation of its 1967 reform.

Differences between the Soviet and Chinese Communist Parties, made public at a Congress of the Rumanian Party in 1960, allowed eastern European states greater latitude in their domestic economic affairs. The declining efficiency of the existing practice was being demonstrated by lower capital productivity and higher ratios of inventories to output or to investment. When the USSR shelved the slogans of Stalin and Khrushchev that the Soviet economy would rapidly 'catch up and surpass the West', eastern European governments acknowledged a lag in living standards and a technological gap in industry. In the early 'sixties, reforms, made possible in the new political climate, had become an economic necessity. Those states which took the Soviet side in the dispute with China made their changes between 1964 and 1968; at the mid-point the USSR undertook its own reform (begun in 1966, largely complete by 1968), amending, but not renouncing, directive centralism. The two which formed their new policy before the Soviet decision—the GDR and Poland —did not abandon directives, but those which decided afterwards—Bulgaria, Czechoslovakia and Hungary—opted for a 'guided-market' solution. From 1960, Albania was aligned with China and Rumania and sought to act as mediator; both dissociated themselves from economic reform: while Albania continues to denounce the new Soviet and east European practices as 'revisionist', Rumania began modest revisions in 1969 for completion during 1970.

The invasion of Czechoslovakia in August 1968 by the USSR and, at its behest, by Bulgaria, the GDR, Hungary and Poland, checked the impetus for change. In April 1969, meeting as delegates to Comecon (the Council for Mutual Economic Assistance), Party and government leaders from the six countries and the USSR resolved upon a form of economic integration which was closer to Soviet preferences than to the 'free-trade area' advocated by Hungary and by Dubček's Czechoslovakia and desired, on political grounds, by Rumania. On the eve of the conference Dubček lost his leadership of the Czechoslovak Communist Party and the political change seems to have been the catalyst—or at least the sign—of a new caution among economic reformers. Hungary remains constant in gearing its new management system to a market, but Bulgaria has deferred new steps and Czechoslovakia has retrogressed.

11

Forms of public management

In the two decades to 1969, four types of socialist industrial administration had been exhibited in eastern Europe. From the viewpoint of the industrial enterprise (the productive unit) two are characterised by operation under instruction from superior authority. The Soviet system, as established in the early 'thirties, is the prototype of such a 'command economy', scrupulously copied in the east Europe of 1950. Prices are used for accounting between enterprises and with them and the government and for regulating the relations of state enterprises with the public—as workers and as buyers of retailed goods. They are not intended, however, to carry information to the enterprise about government or consumers' preferences, which are embodied in plan instructions for input, output, technology and investment during a specified period of time. Albania is the only European state which today embraces that system, although it simplified and decentralised some practices in 1966.

The second form is the variant pioneered by Poland in 1956–8, and now adopted in the GDR, Rumania and the USSR itself. As in the first form the enterprise is set targets for outputs and inputs, and production methods: the goals specified are still numerous, but are everywhere fewer than before; the enterprise has, moreover, some scope to adjust its behaviour to current conditions while fulfilling those targets. Because the interstices of business activity between instructions are large—no goals are set for many functions of the enterprise and some targets may be fulfilled in different ways—attempts are made to use prices to bear information on production, consumption and technique. Such prices are determined by government authority—not regulated by a market—and even so are supplemented or superseded by operational instructions from an intermediate tier of authority, the industrial association, whose creation is also a feature of the second system.

The revised practice places no less importance on compliance with targets, which nevertheless include one on profit, designed to reflect the manager's ability within set limits to adapt his inputs, output and technology in conformity to pre-determined price ratios; rewards are paid (largely from profits earned, though partly from outlays planned as salaries) to the manager and to some or all of his staff when targets are reached, fulfilment of the profit plan being a necessary, but not a sufficient, condition. Such incentives had been available under the earlier version of the 'directive system', but restricted to senior personnel and paid out as part of the wage-bill.

Hungary adopted the third system, a guided market, literally overnight (but after four years' preparation) in 1968. A transitional regime, with some market features, rules in Bulgaria and operated during 1967 and 1968 in Czechoslovakia. In early 1969, a law which would have moved the Czechoslovak system onto the Hungarian plane was on the verge of enactment but was abandoned after the political changes of April. The demarcation at the enterprise level of a guided market system from directive practice lies in the replacement of target fulfilment by direct dependence on revenue and costs. The Czechoslovak or Hungarian enterprise is left to operate re-spectively on value-added or profit; the Bulgarian relies on value-added for wages and self-finance, but has to comply with imposed directives. Value-added, termed 'gross revenue', is the sum of profit and wages, and was for two years in Czecho-slovakia and continuingly in Bulgaria the basis for business taxation, on the model adopted in the tax harmonisation of the European Common Market; Czechoslovakia transferred the liability to profits (as in British fiscal practice) in 1969. For the two years of Czechoslovak transition the central authorities stopped issuing directives on the fulfilment of which incen-tives would depend, but enterprises were insulated from the action of the market by the intervention of industrial associa-tions which re-distributed profit. For a transitional period in Bulgaria, envisaged for three years but extended for at least a further year, industrial associations imposed targets while the central authorities encouraged competition. Prices play an active part in the third model because the market, whence price ratios (and hence profits) derive, has some part in determining the allocation of resources. At this early stage of departure from the directive system, a number of prices remain controlled (both of current flows and of capital through the rate of interest), while many transactions are withheld from market regulation (by quotas for certain commodities and, above all, by rationing access to investment funds).

Both the reformed directive system and the guided market economy use prices as parameters, in conformity to which the enterprise adjusts its activity, but in the one prices are controlled in accordance with a central plan and in the other they are established by the interplay of government and business decisions. The mechanisms may respectively be termed 'state-parametric' and 'market-parametric'; the original Soviet-type practice is 'non-parametric'. In all three the organisation of the firm is the same; responsibility for the state's assets in the plant is entrusted to a manager (entitled the director), who is appointed by an agency of government and who recruits his staff within certain limits of aggregate remuneration (wage-scales and wage-bill maxima in the first and second systems and by specified relationships between basic wages and bonuses in the third).

The fourth type in eastern European industry—the Yugo-slav—is market-parametric, but vests socialist assets in the 'workers' collective'; its example, as already indicated, has been notably significant at times of political crisis, when the democratic implications of 'worker self-government' were crucially attractive, but has not been introduced into the countries considered in the present study.

If a single word can summarise the leading characteristic relating the enterprise to the political structure in the various systems, the first may be termed bureaucratic, the second technocratic, the third managerial and the fourth syndicalist.

Social forces

The association between political liberalisation and economic decentralisation is, however, neither simple nor direct. The command economy suited a 'monolithic' communist party, for it enabled the government to instruct subordinates at its entire discretion; acceptance of parameters limits that power because a change in one involves the automatic adjustment of activities and other parameters—a process decried as 'spontaneity' precluding the purposive direction of the economy by 'scientific marxism'. The issuance of instructions can—and frequently did—contradict others previously given, but centralised authority allowed the establishment of *ad hoc* priorities to meet each case. The administrative confusion and inefficient use of resources resulting from such particularism clearly increased as the activities of the economy widened, became more interdependent or had greater links with trading decisions abroad (which were of course outside the scope of a national plan). It can reasonably be argued that the Czechoslovak economy was already too integrated and trade-dependent for the directive system ever to have been introduced, whereas the industrially less-developed countries— Albania, Bulgaria and Rumania—could gain some advantage from a decisive concentration of resources on objectives which the dispersed choices of a small market economy had failed to achieve. A similar proposition in the sphere of prewar politics contrasts the democracy of Czechoslovakia with dictatorships of varying hue, under which every other country of the region eventually fell.

Political liberalisation—as with Poland in 1956 and Czechoslovakia in 1968—reinforces any trend towards economic decentralisation, but the latter has not by itself induced political change. The reforms in Czechoslovakia in 1958 or in Hungary a decade later, or those of the mid-sixties in Bulgaria, the GDR and Poland, were not stages in political development, and it is by no means certain that, in introducing a guided market economy in January 1967, the

Novotný–Lenárt administration sowed seeds of its fall twelve months afterwards. Checks to the relaxation of political centralism have, on the other hand, held back corresponding steps in the economic mechanism; this has been evident enough in the Hungary of 1956 and the Czechoslovakia of 1969, and may be playing a part in the postponement of economic changes announced in Bulgaria and Rumania for 1968 and 1969 respectively.

The absence of an unequivocal relationship, either way, between the forms of political and economic administration may be partially explained in terms of the interest groups urging or opposing economic reform. The groups were engendered by a common politico-economic centralisation during two decades, but have aligned themselves differently in the various countries of eastern Europe. If analysis—outside the scope of the present work—is to be made of the conjunction of forces which have transformed east European economic organisation from uniformity to disparity in a dozen years, the examination must start with patterns of professional cohesion—notably among Party functionaries, civil servants, factory managers, technicians, financial officials, research staffs, academic economists and trade unionists. The homogeneity of the early 'fifties, on the other hand, was of uniquely political origin.

2
Nationalisation and Central Planning

COPYING STALIN'S five-year plans of the 'thirties, the communist governments which took power in post-war eastern Europe made industrialisation the principal aim of their economic policy, and state management the means. Until then untested outside the Soviet borders, the central planning of industry was probably easier to introduce in their countries than anywhere else on the Continent: before the Second World War the market mechanism had been less effective than in the West and the replacement by directives of an active price system had to that extent been prepared.

The accompanying political revolution was nonetheless complete. Six countries of the area were brought into the orbit of the USSR by the Soviet Army which liberated Czechoslovakia and Poland from the German forces and occupied Eastern Germany and the Axis co-belligerents (Bulgaria, Hungary and Rumania); two others, Albania and Yugoslavia, came by a communist victory in civil war.

The adoption by the Yugoslav government of the Soviet system of central economic planning was immediate, but was as rapidly eclipsed. Industry was nationalised earlier and more fully, and a five-year plan on the Soviet pattern was sooner introduced in Yugoslavia than in any other eastern European state. The exclusion in 1948 of the Yugoslav Communist Party from the Cominform (the successor to the pre-war Comintern, with fewer members but as much an instrument of Soviet policy) eliminated for the government of Marshal Tito the political desirability of imitating the Soviet economy. The trade embargo imposed by Cominform members aggravated the economic misfortunes of excessive centralism and unbalanced industrialisation; from 1952 Yugoslavia began to dismantle its Soviet practices. Albania adopted Soviet principles of industrial administration as soon as change in its simple agrarian structure permitted, but haphazardly until a unified practice was instituted in 1956: alienated from the USSR by its alliance with the China of Mao Tse-tung in 1961, it declined to follow the pattern of reform set by the USSR and the rest of eastern Europe in the mid-'sixties.

The six states which are the principal subject of this study are allied in both a political and an economic respect. The demise of the Cominform in 1956 was compensated by the signing of the Warsaw Treaty in 1955: the military and political alliance is now confined to the USSR and the six countries, for Albania withdrew its membership (purely formal since 1961) in September 1968 in protest against the invocation of the Treaty for the occupation of Czechoslovakia. The economic grouping of Comecon (founded in 1949) does not coincide quite so precisely because, besides the USSR, Albania remains a member (albeit nominally) and Mongolia was introduced in 1962. Membership of the two organisations represents a formal reason for examination as a group, but the practical, though not an exclusive, criterion is common adoption of collective or state ownership of the means of production and a communist party which monopolises political power. Soviet industrial practice need not be separately discussed, but its example was dominant until the middle 'sixties.

Pre-war protection and cartels

In the first decade of the twentieth century nearly all these countries belonged to large empires: Poland was divided between Tsarist Russia, Imperial Germany and Austro-Hungary. The Austro-Hungarian empire incorporated all that is now Czechoslovakia, much of Rumania and the more developed regions of Yugoslavia; the Turkish empire had earlier been forced to yield independence to Bulgaria, Rumania and Serbia, but retained Albania and parts of present-day Bulgaria and Yugoslavia. While the economy of the Ottoman domains was stagnant, industry was being created elsewhere in central and eastern Europe within the tariff boundaries of major multinational states: protective customs duties set up in the latter decades of the nineteenth century permitted the establishment of large-scale manufacturing for big and rapidly developing home markets. Russia, industrialising from 1890 onwards under the direction of the state, took Polish textiles; modern Hungarian flour mills supplied all of Austro-Hungary, the weaving industry of which was concentrated in Bohemia, and the spinning sector in Austria.

The break-up of the empires in 1918 bequeathed parts of industries, serving much larger markets, to small states wherein national sentiments had been released after long constriction: Slovakia had been part of Hungary for nearly a millennium, Bohemia governed by Austria for three centuries, and Poland partitioned for 130 years. To maintain existing industry within a smaller market and to substitute for products previously bought from other parts of each Empire, the countries of the area enacted outright import prohibitions and tariffs of unprecedented severity. In 1921, for example, the Hungarian government imposed an embargo on specified textiles, machinery and leather goods, and raised customs duties as a whole from 10–20 per cent of import value to 30 per cent (in the case of many consumers' goods to 50 per cent); by 1924 Hungary was importing from countries formerly part of the Empire only forty per cent of the volume bought in 1913. The Rumanian tariff was increased on no less than six occasions between 1918 and 1928, and export duties on raw materials sought to foster domestic manufacturing.

The world economic crisis of 1931–3 was keenly felt in the meagre domestic markets of eastern Europe. Even in comfortably-developed Czechoslovakia industrial closures and disastrous unemployment in some measure prepared the country for radical post-war changes out of character with its political history.

The effect of high protection was threefold: it weakened competitive pricing within each domestic market, it encouraged the formation of national cartels and it favoured state intervention and control. In the late 'thirties clearing arrangements with Nazi Germany gave further impetus to economic *dirigisme*; under the strain of the Depression and of a movement of political power from parliamentary government to authoritarianism, the part played by the state in the control of the economy increased.

The environment conducive to cartelisation was equally favourable to the growth of the public ownership of industrial assets: railways, some branches of heavy industry, and the traditional monopolies in tobacco and alcohol were government-operated; utilities and local transport were developed by municipal authorities.

Industry outside the public sector and the protected cartels tended to be very small in scale and run as one-man or family businesses; in the Danubian states other than Czechoslovakia foreign companies were the major entrepreneurs. The capital market was generally underdeveloped and, foreign investment apart, a few large banks played a major role in industrial finance.

The emergency conditions of the war—whether a national government continued (Hungary, Rumania, Bulgaria and Slovakia) or whether enemy occupation prevailed (Poland, the Czech lands and Albania)—greatly increased state intervention. This was exercised through price and other controls, imposition of government-sponsored industrial associations, compulsory procurement of farm produce, rationing of both producers' and consumers' goods and foreign-trade and exchange restrictions. Although the war economy within Germany did not reach the degree of centralisation achieved in the United Kingdom, its control over the peripheral territories virtually liquidated a market economy. The expropriation of Allied assets everywhere, and the imposition of compulsory German administration in much of the industry on occupied territory, made further inroads on the private sector.

Aftermath of war

In the four years following the end of hostilities east and central Europe underwent profound institutional change as political groups other than communist were excluded from effective power. Single-party states were formed behind communist party mergers with the social-democratic party, and unequal coalitions with peasant, Christian-democratic and liberal groups; the junior partners were required to abandon separate economic programmes and opposition to economic, as to any other government, policy came to be voiced only underground or in emigration. Domestic political consolidation—dictated by Stalin in the conditions of Cold War with the West and ideological hostility to Yugoslav heresy—enabled the administration to manage the economy as it chose.

Post-war circumstances further facilitated state management. Everywhere the new governments established in the wake of the victorious Soviet armies enacted laws on agrarian reform and nationalisation. These laws were not entirely copies of Soviet decrees, and, as products of coalitions, left considerably more resources in individual hands than in the USSR. Enough capitalist industry was left in the GDR— the government of which was established in the Soviet zone of Germany in 1949—for 92,000 workers still to be employed in private industry in 1967, while private firms with state-equity shareholders (*halbstaatlich*) produced one-tenth of global industrial output, with a staff of 350,000. The Polish nationalisation law of 1946 declared that enterprises employing up to fifty persons were exempt from nationalisation; similarly the Hungarian nationalisation laws of 1948 and 1949, of Czechoslovakia (1945 and 1948), Bulgaria (1946 and 1947), and Rumania (1948) specified upper limits for exemption. Only in Albania—in the words of the official *History of the Albanian Party of Labour*—was 'socialisation effected rapidly and in a deeply revolutionary way on the basis of confiscation without compensation'. At later dates, in the manner of the Soviet Constitution of 1936, some, though not all, Civil Codes were drafted so as virtually to exclude capitalist industrial enterprise.

Nowhere has land been nationalised, and the post-war reforms allowed fairly large private holdings. In Poland, for example, farms could be as large as 50 hectares in the eastern and up to 100 hectares in the western regions (mostly those areas taken over from Germany); holdings as large as 50 hectares could be retained in Rumania, provided the owner had farmed the land himself over the seven years preceding the decree. In general only large, well-run capitalist farms and royal or ecclesiastical land were taken over by the state. The effective rights of private agriculture were, however, short-lived: two waves of government-sponsored collectivisation—around 1950 and 1960—brought most farmland into co-operatives. Unlike the Soviet *kolkhoz*, the area brought into a co-operative remains formally the property of the members. The only exceptions to peasant collectivisation are small plots around the homestead, and agriculture in Poland where private farming overwhelmingly prevails.

The rights of private industry were still more rapidly extinguished: within two or three years nearly all the plants which had ostensibly been exempt from expropriation were in government hands. Shortage of managerial personnel and a policy of rationalisation would in any case have dictated some concentration of management, while many firms were taken under state management because their owners were no longer there to run them. The Nazi massacre of Jews had liquidated many factory and business proprietors; emigration to Israel in 1948–50 reduced Bulgarian Jewry to a mere 5000, one-tenth of its pre-war size; one in ten of the pre-war Polish population had been Jewish, but only 80,000 were left after the war. The expulsion of Germans from western Poland, eastern Prussia, Sudetenland and Transylvania and the exchange of minorities between Slovakia and Hungary left

22

many enterprises without a head; the only post-war migration which had no effect on industrial management was the expulsion by Bulgaria of 155,000 Turks, farmers and traders, in 1950–1.

In the ex-enemy countries, Bulgaria, Rumania and Hungary, German and Austrian assets were transferred to Soviet ownership by the 1947 Peace Treaty. Under the Potsdam Agreement of 1945 the USSR was authorised to dismantle key plant in the Soviet zone of Germany; although sizeable shipments went to the USSR, most was allowed to remain *in situ* and was operated as a Soviet enterprise (*sowjetische aktiengesellschaft*, abbreviated to SAG). Jointly with a compulsory contribution from the national authorities, Soviet assets in Bulgaria, Rumania and Hungary were set up as 'mixed companies', forming the core of a state sector in advance of broad nationalisation. Two 'mixed companies' were established by agreement in Czechoslovakia.

The special relationship with the USSR contributed to centralisation along two other paths—the emergence of the Soviet Union as a dominant trade partner and its political pressure to copy the Soviet model.

The USSR had operated a foreign-trade monopoly since 1918 and centralised economic management since its first five-year plan (1928–32). With increasing deliveries to and from the Soviet Union, east European governments had to negotiate with a foreign-trade monopoly and to undertake the long-term trade agreements upon which their partner insisted; those which had been enemies were required to deliver reparations, the procurement of which involved government intervention in commerce, carried back to the control of suppliers.

The political monoliths established when coalitions had served their purpose followed the Soviet example in displaying hostility towards private economic initiative. Collectivisation expressed this policy in agriculture; industrial enterprises below the nationalisation limits were forced into liquidation by penal taxation, by denial of supplies and finance from nationalised factories and banks, by exclusion of access to

23

foreign customers and by the prohibition of private dealings in foreign exchange. Services ancillary to industry were similarly treated. There was no outright nationalisation of domestic trade, a few big stores and wholesalers apart. Government agencies ('material-technical supply organisations') were given preference over private wholesalers in the transactions of nationalised enterprises; municipal and co-operative stores pre-empted goods away from private shopkeepers, although a few managed to survive, selling non-rationed items (consumer rationing persisted in Albania and the GDR until 1958), until their numbers were augmented under government favour in the mid-'sixties. The independent professionals serving industry—lawyers, draughtsmen, surveyors, etc.—were either recruited by state agencies or pressed into co-operatives; financial offices of all kinds were nationalised with banking, insurance and foreign-exchange dealing, and functions such as real estate and stockbroking lost their *raison d'être*. By 1950 state ownership of the means of production was virtually complete, peasant farming only excepted. When in 1954 the Soviet Union renounced reparations and made over its share in mixed companies, national-government ownership was unified.

Central planning and autonomous management

Abrupt as may seem the changes of 1946–50, coalitions and single-party administrations alike had made some attempt to build upon post-war controls and emergency measures a structure of state ownership which shared features both of the Soviet economy and of planning as it was then being practised in western Europe. The countries were all seen as open to trade and steps were soon taken to allow nationalised industries to negotiate their projections with those of other planned economies. Farther reaching than OEEC plan co-operation (1949–53) under the impetus of Marshall Aid, joint planning commissions and sub-committees were being created by east European neighbours in 1946–8 (Czechoslovakia–Poland, Czechoslovakia–Hungary, Albania–Yugoslavia, Bulgaria–Yugoslavia, Bulgaria–Rumania and Hungary–Yugoslavia); their end, however, was spelled in a damning *Pravda* editorial of 28 January 1948. The 'national reconstruction plans' of Poland and of Hungary (each 1947–9) and of Czechoslovakia (1947–8) were in many respects forbears of the later 'guided market economy', and were attuned to western European thinking on macro-economic management and public investment. The Polish plan was received as a 'mixture of Marx and Keynes', Kaldor went from Cambridge to help draft the Hungarian plan, and delegates of the French planning commission studied Czechoslovak techniques.

The investment structure of the plans was set up primarily upon projections of demand and nationalised enterprises were accorded considerable latitude in their finance. They everywhere retained, as under joint-stock or personal ownership, their own capital, which could be augmented from profits or by borrowing from banks. Where public money ('programmed investment' under the Czechoslovak Plan, for example) was provided, it was as an increment to the enterprise's own capital: later the Ministry of Finance, through the banking system, was to become a direct paymaster, doling out funds *pari passu* with actual construction work or equipment purchase. Through 'industrial boards' nationalised concerns in some cases had channels for the discussion of plans with ministries and the planning office, which was nowhere shadowed by the hierarchic subordination marking the 'fifties.

The idea of a national plan was not new in eastern Europe. The Hungarian government in March 1938 had published a 'billion pengoe plan', which envisaged the annual expenditure of 200 million pengoes (£8 mn.) for five years as investment subsidies to heavy industry, transport, and agricultural improvement, and two years later a Supreme Economic Council had been set up to co-ordinate its implementation. It was substantially due to capital formation under this plan (more than envisaged) that the number of factory workers rose from 289,000 in 1938 to 392,000 in 1943. Hungary, too, launched a ten-year plan for agriculture in 1941, an investment plan also (100 mn. pengoes annually); its implementation, disrupted by the War, was less significant than that of the industrial plan. The Hungarian plans had much in common with a regional plan for the Central Industrial District ('COP') in Poland, involving state investment grants for the establishment of new industrial plant. In Rumania a Supreme Council for the Administration of Public Property and Enterprises was created as early as 1929 to co-ordinate the current and capital operations of the public sector.

The post-war plans were novel because they were intended to influence productive activity as a whole. Scholars from east Europe had been prominent before the War in developing marxian socialism, and were influential after it in their homelands in establishing a justification for planning independent of strictly Soviet influence. Among many economists, Lange and Kalecki went back from the USA and the UK to Poland. Vajda, who had spent the war in London, became President of the Hungarian Planning Commission and Lukács, the philosopher, returned from Moscow to Budapest. The Czechoslovak Central Planning Commission which drafted the first Five-year plan in 1948 was a powerful combination of intellectual talent, drawing upon pre-war business (Outrata, the Chairman, was formerly the Director-General of Zbrojovka, the light-armaments firm at Brno which produced the Bren gun), communists (Frejka), social democrats (Maiwald) and national socialists (Šlechta): Gottwald, the communist Prime Minister, called the Commission 'the catalyst of the National Front'.

The Soviet pattern

Much of the intellectual impetus, and all national individualities, disappeared from eastern European planning as political control by, and within, each communist party came to be forcibly modelled upon Stalin's practice.

A distinctive feature of the Soviet system was the detailed planning of production and its distribution in physical units, with some aggregation of those units in money terms, either as a convenient form of representing quantities or where the specification of items in their own measures was considered a scrupulosity. Quantification in physical terms represented magnitudes that the political leaders could readily comprehend. Purges among state and political officials during 1948–52 swept away many of those capable of more sophisticated economics in policy-making. The deterioration in the quality of government economic thinking was similar to that accompanying the purge of the Soviet State Planning Commission by Kuibyshev and the arraignment on political charges of leading economic officials, in high repute in the West, during 1930–1: in eastern Europe the changes were associated with the disgrace of Gomulka in Poland, and the trials and imprisonment of Slansky in Czechoslovakia, Pătrăşcanu in Rumania, Rajk in Hungary and Kostov in Bulgaria. As the government of the GDR was constituted by the USSR only in 1949, its membership conformed to Stalin's requirements from the start. The technique of 'material balances'—planning output and its disposal in units of physical measurement —not only reduced the formulation of goals to simple terms, but was susceptible of manipulation in governmental practice: a process of bargaining which may be termed 'administrative iteration' (see page 67), whereby ministers for the industries concerned or other political authorities negotiated for supplies, became the standard practice for evolving the outline of the central plan.

The delineation of plan goals in physical terms was accompanied by a similar classification of the process of production and distribution. Industrial enterprises were grouped by product and subordinated to 'central administrations' which were components of an industrial ministry. The wider the range of national production, the larger was the number of such ministries, each concerned with a specific branch of industry. The pattern of industrial ministries did not subsequently vary as extensively as in the USSR, where the three post-war decades saw almost continual division, merger, re-division,

27

dissolution and re-establishment of branch-specialist ministries. After an initial period of experiment (until about 1957), and, with some slight expansion as the development of new branches justified, the number of ministries was relatively stable and, in comparison with the USSR, fairly modest. Thus in 1969, when there were forty-three industrial ministries in the USSR, there were ten in Rumania, eight in the GDR and Poland, six in Bulgaria, four in Hungary, and only one in Albania and Czechoslovakia (see Appendix, page 161). These ministries, other relevant departments of state and the Central Committee Secretariat of each communist party may collectively be defined as the 'central authorities'.

The organisation of the economy was thus hierarchical, and decision-making was concentrated very close to the top of the pyramid. Requests for a decision, together with the information needed, were passed up the chain of command and instructions were sent down. Because the planning process was expected to be comprehensive, and in order to ensure that sufficient data were available for the resolution of interdepartmental conflict and the issuance of planning orders, more information was demanded than could be utilised. At a rough estimate, only one-fifth of data submitted was, in fact, used for planning purposes, while statistics needed for rational planning went uncomputed—the national accounts of Czechoslovakia, for example, were not estimated during the early years of the First Five-year Plan.

The direction of subordinate bodies, including industrial enterprises, was chiefly effected through direct administrative order. This required that inferiors contact each other through their respective superiors. Once such contact had been established, the relationships laid down tended to persist, simply because of the difficulty of re-negotiation. The system also involved the rationing of the means of production: materials were allocated by limiting both demand and supply, and employment maxima were established on the demand side, that is, the enterprise was allowed a quota of specified current inputs and capital equipment and could recruit manpower only within a specified wage-bill. This form of direct rationing was accompanied by a financial control which may be translated as 'business accountability' (or 'economic accountability', 'cost accounting'): derived from a Russian acronym, *khozraschet* was essentially the imposition of a constraint on enterprise in fulfilling other directives that average cost be no greater than average revenue. Planned losses would be covered by a budget subsidy, and planned profits were subject to re-allocation by the Ministry of Finance and sometimes within the industrial ministry itself.

The main stress in assessing enterprise plan fulfilment was, however, always on the quantitative results rather than on the economic or financial aspects of operation. Managerial incentives (bonuses payable to the factory director and his senior staff) were tied to indicators measured in global value. At the operative level, piece-rates (and especially progressive piece-rates, whereby exact fulfilment and over-fulfilment of a planned task were remunerated more highly than under-fulfilment) were the equivalent for workers, but for them there was very little participation by premia tied to enterprise operation. Both managerial and operative groups benefited in a very small way from profits through the 'directors' fund' (pages 110–17) and a few premia were paid for notable collective achievements in 'socialist emulations'. The widespread use of material incentives for managers, based upon plan fulfilment, and the issuance of administrative orders supplementing the plan targets, conduced to a complicated pattern of trade-offs between the various instructions and rules and the monetary rewards for fulfilment or adherence.

Of three tenets of Soviet administrative practice, one was invariably followed, viz. that at each level of the administrative hierarchy a single person should be in charge: 'one-man rule' was the practice derived from Soviet usage under the early Five-year Plans, but such 'line management' has frequently, if informally, been vitiated by 'functional' intrusions, when specialist agencies (finance, prices, trade, labour, etc.) have bypassed the hierarchical order. The second principle, of 'dual subordination'—whereby an enterprise is subject to a local as well as to a central agency—is rarer in eastern Europe: it has regularly been used in the GDR and Poland and for certain periods in Albania, Hungary and Rumania. A third, 'collegiality' in higher administrative bodies—consultative committees of department heads and certain senior staff in a ministry ('collegium') or research institute ('scientific council'), was adopted during the 'fifties after Soviet emphasis on it was revived by the post-Stalin governments to replace 'the cult of personality' by 'collectivism'.

There were three salient characteristics also for the citizen as worker and as consumer under the Soviet-type economic mechanism. As a worker, he was free to choose his employment, save for a few constraints over limited periods—for university graduates, for example, for a short time after graduation (now abandoned in Czechoslovakia and Hungary). Occasional prohibitions arose for political reasons: persons under suspicion were frequently denied work equal to their capabilities and allowed only junior or menial jobs ('black work' in the Rumanian phrase of the time). Forced labour never reached the magnitude of the Soviet Union during the various purges, but the Danube-Black Sea Canal in Rumania and coal-mining in Hungary were notorious for this in the early 'fifties.

As consumer the individual was free to dispose of his earnings, except that rationing persisted in eastern Europe later than in the West. Moreover, Bulgaria, Czechoslovakia and Poland twice imposed a currency reform (respectively in 1947 and 1952, 1945 and 1953 and 1945 and 1950), whereas only the worst-hit countries of western Europe made a similar, and once-for-all, indent on cash holdings at the end of hostilities (in Germany, 1948). Old banknotes and bank-deposits were renominated in new currency at a scale of rates disfavouring large holders.

Finally, indirect taxation became, after 1949, the basic source of government funds, rising in Bulgaria, for example, from less than one-third to half total revenue. This change conformed to the standard Soviet system of public finance, in which turnover tax and deductions from the profits of state enterprises constitute the bulk of government income. Direct taxation on wages and salaries has been low but has contributed more, and very rarely less, than the 7 to 8 per cent of receipts which it has done since the War in the Soviet Union; the two exceptions are Albania since 1956 (following a policy which by now has all but extinguished direct taxation) and Rumania since 1960 (where it constitutes around 5 per cent of revenue).

A 'war economy'

The Soviet system adopted in east Europe was termed by Lange, the Polish economist, '*sui generis* a war economy'. Its installation took place against a background of threatening hostilities: the Korean War, the NATO embargo on deliveries to eastern Europe of strategic and similar goods, and counter-measures by Comecon members led the governments of eastern Europe towards physical allocations. Shortages of food and manufactures and failure to control wages induced inflationary pressure which was met by severe consumer rationing. UNRRA supplies, which had rehabilitated the war-torn economies of Europe, ceased in 1946; whereas western Europe enjoyed Marshall Aid, eastern Europe had a net obligation towards the Soviet Union. The USSR made some deliveries on credit at moments of emergency, but it was far offset by reparations deliveries and adverse terms of trade. Shortages of foreign exchange brought the imposition of exchange control and the Western embargo added to the need for import rationing. The practice of bilateral agreements in trade between the eastern European countries and with the USSR, mentioned above, also conduced to a rationing process. Like nationalisation and planning, this was not new; compulsory quotas at prices fixed by inter-state agreement accounted for half of German–Hungarian trade in 1944, and when, in 1947, state-trading arrangements were re-established, there had been little scope in the intermission for the exercise of market relationships.

A combination of handing down orders in military fashion and a bureaucratic preference for referring responsibility upward overwhelmed the central authorities with detail and caused the aggregation of error and misinformation as data were reported and instructions dispatched. Moreover, because the reporting enterprises expected to receive a plan based upon their past returns, they tended to distort their statistics in the fashion which would gain the most favourable plan. There soon came a point, therefore, at which flows between enterprises and even between entire industries were no longer patterned upon rational signals and transactions. The resulting exchanges were so erroneous that no quantitative basis existed for the application of sophisticated planning techniques: the vicious circle has been most evident in prices, relations among which were too distorted to serve as a starting-point for reform.

Employment in the central authorities was never large enough to deal satisfactorily with the decisions required. In the 'fifties the Polish Planning Commission had a staff of 1200; today, staffs are smaller and are likely to be further reduced. The planning office employs 700 in Hungary, 500 in Rumania and 50 in Albania: the establishment of the industrial ministries in Hungary was 7000 in 1968, to be reduced to 5000 as the economic reforms took effect. But—in the absence of today's computer technology—had the numbers expanded to allow rational reflection on each problem, they would have by far exceeded the span of control of the inner group of Party leaders and functionaries who monopolised political power. Some, and on occasion all, of the tasks properly associated with central planning were neglected—to evaluate the potential of the economy, to contribute to the establishment of national objectives, to select that combination of resources and technologies among many which would best achieve the chosen ends, and to negotiate the adjustment of goals, or rearrange the use of productive factors, as unforeseen conditions arise during implementation.

3
Tiers of Authority

INDUSTRY (if defined as manufacturing and mining) is the only branch of the east European economies which is controlled both as to its input and its output by other state organisations, having its sole contact with households (that is, private consumers) through the payment of wages. Under the directive system even this latter contact is limited by the dictation of the size (and even the composition) of wage payments by superior authority. Its links with other branches and with the consumer are in the hands of other nationalised bodies, domestic-retail and foreign-trade organisations, 'material-technical supply' (see page 37) and financial and transport services. The potential for administrative direction is at its most complete in industry and was exploited to the maximum in the early 'fifties.

Except in Albania and Hungary, a four-tier organisation comprises the authorities which formulate national policy and follow its implementation, economic ministries, industrial associations and enterprises. The individual factory may coincide with the enterprise, or be one of many in it, but, by and large, has no more autonomy of the enterprise than has a workshop or section within a factory. The industrial association has never existed in Albania; nor is it any longer a tier of formal state authority in Hungary because compulsory membership has (with some exceptions) been abandoned. Obligatory participation was intended to cease for Czechoslovak enterprises at the beginning of 1970: under draft legislation, now abandoned, an industrial association was to lapse if members had not confirmed their voluntary adherence by the end of the year. From that date, as now generally in Hungary, the association would have given no directives to enterprises and could not therefore be considered part of an administrative hierarchy.

The agencies collectively constituting the central governmental authorities may readily be identified (see Appendix, page 161), but the most important partner in any major decision—and in a considerable number of minor ones—is the secretariat of the ruling party, about the organisation of which virtually nothing is published. The party name may, for convenience, be cited as that used in the USSR—the Communist Party—but it varies from country to country and in some cases from time to time: the Albanian Party of Labour was the Communist Party of Albania from its foundation in 1941 until 1948; the Bulgarian Communist Party was so called between its foundation in 1919 until 1938, when for ten years it went under the name of the Workers' Party; the Communist Party of Czechoslovakia has kept the same title since its establishment in 1921; the Socialist Unity Party in the GDR was formed in 1946 of the Communist and Social Democratic Parties in the Soviet zone of occupation; the Hungarian Socialist Workers' Party was reorganised after the 1956 uprising from the Hungarian Workers' Party, formed in 1948 by a merger of the Communist and Social Democratic Parties; the Polish United Workers' Party was created by a similar fusion in the same year; and the Rumanian Communist Party, established as such in 1921, following its absorption of the Social Democratic Party in 1948, was called the Workers' Party until 1965.

The centre of authority is a small group within the Central Committee, which is elected by delegates to the Party Congress. The economic decisions reached by a Congress tend to be of the broadest nature (e.g. consideration of a five-year plan), but the Rumanian Party, for example, convened a conference (in December 1967) to discuss industrial reform, a function occasionally fulfilled elsewhere by an 'expanded plenary session' of the Party Central Committee. Most important policies have the stamp of the Central Committee, but all significant policy-making is by its Political Bureau

(Politburo). A two-tier variant (and without use of the title Politburo) operates in Czechoslovakia (an Executive Committee being the standing organ of a larger Presidium, to which are delegated powers of the Central Committee) and in Rumania (where the reverse nomenclature is used, a Presidium being formed of a larger Executive Committee of the Central Committee).

Not all the Secretaries of the Party are members of the Politburo, although the Secretary responsible for economic affairs is invariably included; the First Secretary ('General Secretary' in Rumania) is the political leader of the country. Stalin's practice (from the German invasion until his death) of combining the leadership of the Party with Chairmanship of the Council of Ministers (Prime Minister) was once generally copied in eastern Europe, but is now followed only in Bulgaria. The Party Secretaries (the 'Secretariat') have at their disposition a substantial staff (the 'apparatus'), nominally the employees of the Central Committee, but decision-makers of last resort either by delegation from the Politburo, or tacitly, as in Poland by 1968; they are grouped into departments, one or more of which deal with industrial and other economic affairs. The 'Economic Section' of the Rumanian Central Committee was, however, dissolved by a resolution of the Party Conference of December 1967 which required the merger of key party and government administrative offices. Thus the General Secretary of the Party combined his position with that of President of the State Council (head of state), and the Party Secretary for Economic Affairs became Chairman of the Economic Council (and Vice-President of the State Council); a Party and Government Central Commission for Planning was established in 1967 to draft plans for 1975 and 1980, and Party, government and academic economists were appointed as 'economic advisers' to the Council of Ministers. At regional levels of government, the posts of first secretary of the local party committee and chairman of the county council are held by one person, as are those of secretary of a town committee and mayor of a municipal council.

Without personal pluralism in the hierarchies, the other eastern European countries merge decision-making by interlocking memberships of committees and by frequent mutual consultation: the functions of party and government, in economics as in all spheres, are indistinguishable at the highest level.

Planning and control agencies

Constitutionally, the Council of Ministers is as much responsible to a parliamentary assembly as the Politburo is to the Party Congress, but because parliament in every country for twenty years has comprised a majority (or even totality) of communist deputies, all significant decisions revert to the Party organisation. The degree to which economic decisions are taken by individual members of, or collectively by, the Council, varies widely from matter to matter and from country to country, but everywhere economic ministers form what is in the British equivalent a 'Cabinet Committee'. Bulgaria, Czechoslovakia and Rumania have recently formed distinct 'Economic Councils' comprising both ministers and outside experts, in two cases as a government commission and in Rumania as a joint organ of the Party Central Committee and the State Council. Similar councils had existed in the GDR and Poland (as in the contemporary USSR) but were dissolved at the end of 1965 and 1962 respectively.

Following Soviet practice, the State Planning Commission (under the slightly differing titles listed in the Appendix) is formally an advisory agency of the Council of Ministers, but early gained *de facto* executive functions. It was to signify the Commission's grading to equality with other departments that it was renamed a 'Ministry' in the overhaul of the Czechoslovak Government in April 1968; in the Hungarian reform that January the executive usages of the National Planning Office were withdrawn; and since November 1969 in Rumania the Committee is empowered to propose only draft plans to ministries.

The Commission is divided into 'synthesis' and 'branch'

departments: the former deal with such cross-sector subjects as investment, finance, prices, manpower and wages, and are headed by a co-ordination department which is, in effect, the core of the detailed planning process; only Departments for Plan Coordination and for Development remain in the Rumanian Committee. The degree of intimacy between its own and the specialist departments of the Central Committee is a matter of conjecture, but there is certainly much exchange between the planning commission and the ministries, which, in turn, may be classed as dealing with 'synthesis', with a specific branch, or with 'control'. The minimum for agencies of synthesis is found in Albania: a Ministry of Finance, and a Committee on Labour and Prices. Two such bodies, together with another to oversee research policy, are elsewhere the standard. Branch ministries for industry are paralleled by others for agriculture, building, transport, communications and foreign and domestic trade: the two latter are combined in Albania and there is no ministry dealing with domestic trade in Czechoslovakia.

The principal agent of 'control' (in a sense derived from the Russian for 'verifying', e.g. the fulfilment of any government order) is the banking system, whence the adoption in every country—with the currency suitably altered—of 'control by the rouble', viz. that the execution of planned movements of goods and services would be checked by a corresponding bank entry. Direct control over those movements is exercised by the material-technical supply system, mainly under the Planning Commission but partly or residually operating under separate bodies in Bulgaria, the GDR and Hungary. The statistical office, which under the directive system publishes a plan fulfilment report for each year—and in most cases half-year—determines the form of statistical reporting, by enterprises and ministries, collecting some data directly from plan executants and other aggregates from the supervising ministries. Albania, Bulgaria, the GDR and Hungary retain a fourth line of 'control' in a government agency of that name or as a 'workers' and 'peasants' inspectorate'. The model is the early Soviet Workers' and Peasants' Inspectorate, now the USSR Commission on State Control, the terms of reference of which are to 'verify expenditure of funds and assets in order to control the fulfilment of government decisions by economic organisations and enterprises, and to strengthen state discipline'.

Poland, which in 1956 was the first country to deviate from the strict Soviet model of industrial administration, then replaced its Ministry of State Control by a Supreme Chamber of Control under parliamentary authority. A similar change was made in Rumania in 1968 when the Controlul de Stat was taken over by the Economic Council (nominated by parliament through the State Council, not by the government); a branch of the Ministry of Finance created in 1948 —the Revizor General—remained, as elsewhere in eastern Europe, as government auditor. Hungary dropped its Ministry of State Control in 1957 and established a Central Committee for Popular Supervision, which has only a small staff and investigates cases by committee appointment *ad hoc*; in the reforms of a decade later it also withdrew direct auditing authority from the Ministry of Finance by transferring that function to a new, semi-autonomous office, the Revenue Administration.

The banking system

The Rumanian audit in 1968 examined 400,000 accounts held by 22,000 entities, but the basic execution of the financial plan is, on standard east European practice, in the hands of the banks.

Within three years of the end of the war, all eastern European banks had been nationalised, including the central bank where, as in Czechoslovakia, Hungary and Rumania, it had previously been a joint-stock company with state participation. The first country to undertake nationalisation was Czechoslovakia which, in October 1945, nationalised the National Bank and all large commercial banks; banks were nationalised in Albania in 1946, in Bulgaria and Hungary in

38

1947 and in Poland and Rumania in 1948 (their National Banks having already been placed under state control in 1945 and 1946 respectively): the remaining private banks in Czechoslovakia were compulsorily merged during 1948 into two publicly-owned banks for short-term credit (the Živnostenská Bank and, for Slovakia, the Tatra Bank), but when a new State Bank of Czechoslovakia was established in 1950 the National Bank and these two institutions lost their identity (the Živnostenská Bank being, however, re-established in 1956, with a branch in London for trade and private dealings). In the Soviet Zone of Germany the military government transferred the branches of the Reichsbank and all large commercial banks to newly-established small regional banks operating as public enterprises; a similar programme was followed in the Western Zone in a process which, in accordance with Potsdam policy, dismantled the national banking structure in favour of local banks on the United States model. An anomalous situation existed in the areas of the Eastern Zone originally occupied by United States forces, where certain small banks continued to operate after the districts had been taken over by the Soviet Army; with one exception, in Leipzig, these were eventually nationalised in 1953.

After the monetary reform in 1948, and in parallel with the creation of the Bank Deutsche Länder in the Western Zones (subsequently the Deutsche Bundesbank), a Deutsche Emissions und Girobank (later the Deutsche Notenbank and now the Staatsbank) was established in the Soviet Zone. Because Berlin, under the Potsdam Agreements, formed part of no Zone, separate banking institutions were established for the former capital, but the chief of these, the Berliner Stadtkontor, soon became *de facto* a branch of the Notenbank.

Apart from their function as bank of issue, the central banks of eastern Europe manage the government account on behalf of the Ministry of Finance, and those of all state enterprises. Co-operatives can in some instances hold their accounts at the central bank but in others are directed to specialised institutions, e.g. in the GDR the Bank for Artisans and Craftsmen, and in Poland the Association of Savings and Loan Co-operatives; private individuals may bank with the various savings banks, mostly pre-war foundations in which some additional banking activities have been instituted explicitly to preclude the need for private accounts (small-scale industry apart) at the central bank.

Except in Albania and Czechoslovakia, it was found a convenience for long-term investment grants to be channelled through a specialised investment bank instead of through the central bank. Because in all seven countries payments were non-reimbursable and bore no interest there was no need for expertise on creditworthiness and solvency, but specialisation had the advantage of establishing an inspectorate, composed chiefly of engineers and other technicians, to examine on each construction site (or in a factory being extended) the progress of translating investment funds into real assets. The bank does not authorise the payment of a subsequent *tranche* of the finance until it is satisfied that current outlays are maintaining the planned pace of construction and installation. Although, again for convenience, the investment banks furnished short-term credit to construction enterprises, the bulk of working capital, partly interest-bearing loans, was channelled through the central bank. With the continuing exception of Albania (and only recently in Czechoslovakia and Rumania), a specialist foreign-trade bank was also established, mainly to bring together the experts for such transactions.

Local authorities

Some publicly-owned industrial plants are run by a regional or local authority, which also has the oversight of co-operative or private handicrafts and small-scale industry and, usually, of any industrial processing undertaken by co-operative or private farms.

The GDR has the most extensive network of local management, which comprises almost as many industrial

40

units as are managed nationally (although, being each smaller on average, their output is only one-sixth of the total). A VVB(B) or a VVB(K) is formed at the *Bezirk* or *Kreis* level where the number of enterprises warrants, on the model of the VVB(Z), the national industrial association (see page 43) with the Z for *Zentrale*. 'Half-state' enterprises are grouped as their scale of operation indicates, and state enterprises may be dually-subordinate to the local authority and to a ministry for such industry.

Both Poland and Rumania have commissions attached to the level of government immediately below the central (respectively the *województwo* and the *judet*) which are entitled to receive reports from ministry-run enterprises as well as to run their own local factories and services. Plants operated by Polish local authorities are also subordinated to the appropriate industrial association at the national level, as well as being formed into the equivalent of such an association for themselves. Like its national counterpart (see page 36), the Rumanian local economic commission functions as an agent both of the government and of the party.

The Czechoslovak federal constitution of 1969 inserted a new set of administrations between central (now federal) and regional (*kraj*) bodies in the form of ministries for the Czech Lands and for Slovakia. The *kraj* was in 1969 eliminated as superfluous in Slovakia, and the creation is likely, both there and in the Czech Lands, of a new unit which would be larger than the *okres*, the lowest-level authority now managing industrial plant. Fifteen per cent of industrial firms are 'local' (but with 4 per cent of industrial employment).

In Hungary 'local industry' was until the 1968 reform subject both to the regional authority (*megye*) and to the relevant industrial ministry, but this dual subordination has since been abolished. Because a central feature of the new mechanism is the regulations and taxes on profits (see pages 122–5) special procedures are applied to co-operatives to equalise their position vis-à-vis state concerns. Handicraft co-operatives pay the 'tax' to their federation (which is de-subsidised by the amount received), while co-operative farms making industrial products pay turnover tax at a rate increased to a point equivalent to the fiscal burdens borne by a state enterprise.

The supervision of virtually all industry in Bulgaria was decentralised to the region (*okrug*) in 1959, but industrial ministries were subsequently re-established with, again, 'local industry' left to the regional or municipal authority. Handicraft co-operatives in 1969 were merged into a national organisation with retail co-operatives. In Albania, smaller enterprises are run by the local (*rreth*) authority, which, while within the purview of the State Planning Commission, has had a freer hand since the dissolution of the Ministry of Local Economy in 1966, and has never been subject to the Ministry of Industry and Mining. The latter, on the other hand, took over the Union of Handicraft Co-operatives in 1967 (its chairman becoming a Deputy Minister). A similar procedure was applied to the Union of Consumer Co-operatives with respect to the Ministry of Trade.

Industrial associations

Dissatisfaction with a hierarchy of ministries for centralised management of industry began to emerge in the mid-fifties. In 1957 Soviet industrial ministries were abolished and their plants were transferred to regional agencies, 'councils of the national economy' (*sovnarkhozy*); 'local industry' remained subordinate to the region (*oblast*), district (*raion*) or town. The corresponding move in the east Europe of the time (Bulgaria's 'regionalisation' of 1959 excepted) was to devolve authority in altogether a different direction, namely to the industrial branch. The new 'industrial associations' were created from the branch-specialised 'central administrations' of the ministries, and appeared first in Poland (by a decree of April 1958), although they did not wrest from the ministries substantive control over their enterprises until 1966. The staff of the former ministerial administration tended to become automatically that of the new industrial association, but even in the earliest cases the change had a deeper meaning than administrative convenience.

There was a clear intention to form socialist corporations not dissimilar to the public corporations of capitalist countries, exemplified in the Coal Board, British Railways, the BBC, or the Post Office in the United Kingdom. The new tier of management was an effort to transform the intermediate levels of the industrial hierarchy from a bureaucratic to a business basis: the new industrial associations were put on 'business accountability' and bonuses began to be paid to their staff on the basis of the performance of enterprises subordinate to the association: the central administrations had been supported by public funds in the same way as any other department of government.

The official view was that industrial associations were a compromise between maintaining central control and allowing initiative to the individual enterprise. But the double responsibility thus put on an association left unclear whether it was to act as a business corporation or a department of state. In the event the balance of choice between the two functions emerged differently in each country.

The Polish 'association' in its first ten years best exhibited the traits of this ambiguity: as described below (page 93) it would be the advocate of its constituents during plan formation, but would serve as the agent of the ministry in plan implementation. Czechoslovak associations (which have had a variety of titles: 'productive-economic unit' is currently predominant) when they began to emerge after 1958 were more cartels of their enterprises, jointly representing them to the supervising ministry, but the latter was too powerful, until 1967, for them to have much effect, and dissatisfaction among enterprise managers with the ministry spread to disavowal of the association. Authority to leave an association, originally planned for the end of 1969, has not, however, been granted. The Bulgarian 'state economic amalgamation' is modelled on Czechoslovak practice and has not resolved the dichotomy of commercial autonomy and government agency. The GDR created the 'amalgamation of people's enterprises' (VVB) in 1964 and endowed it, rather than constituent enterprises, with the business function. Among the countries continuing the directive system, its authority vis-à-vis the ministry is the most extensive.

Rumanian ministries were relatively late (1952) in gaining authority to draw up the detail of their enterprises' plans without scrutiny from the planning office and other departments of party and government. It was perhaps partly for this reason that Rumanian ministries have been the last to yield power to the 'central offices' (200 of which, covering all industry save food-processing, were established between April and November 1969), devolving upon them fewer powers than in any other eastern European state. The one significant step was that effective in 1970 whereby associations distribute budget investment grants to their enterprises. It goes without saying that, no economic reform having been introduced, there are no associations in Albania, where industrial enterprises are subordinate either directly to the Ministry of Industry and Mining, or, as just described, to the executive committee of the region.

The Hungarian 'union' which came into existence in 1968 differs radically from associations in other east European countries and has more antecedents. Its historical origin may be traced to the 'industrial boards' of private and public enterprises in the main individual branches, compulsorily established just after the war, and which, following nationalisation, were replaced not only by the standard 'central administration' of a ministry but in a few cases, from 1950 onwards, by 'trusts'; both directed their enterprises as a convenient intermediate tier of the hierarchy. Trusts with a more commercial orientation began to be established experimentally in 1959 and a major reorganisation effected during 1963 virtually replaced the central administration either by a trust or by a 'large enterprise' (the much smaller autonomy of the constituent factory in the latter distinguished it from the former). In 1968 the 'central administration' was finally

44

eliminated, but the 'large enterprises' remained and only a few trusts were broken up (although constituent enterprises were empowered to change the internal structure of the trust as commercial efficiency required). Moreover, parallel to the continuance of earlier types of association, a new form, the 'union', was allowed as a technical and servicing unit without the separate business activity of a trust. While a 'union' can be compulsorily established (but in that case only for a maximum period of five years), it is intended to be a novel form of voluntary enterprise co-operation without tendencies to monopoly power externally and bureaucracy internally.

Division by accountability

The industrial hierarchy under the reformed directive system may be classified into two broad categories, the 'central authorities' on the one hand, which formulate the plans and oversee their performance, and 'plan executants', the function of which is to implement the plan, though without excluding a contributory role for executants in plan formulation. A criterion may be found in the principle of business accountability, which places agencies financed through the government budget, viz. the planning commission, industrial ministries, and certain other supervisory bodies, as the central authorities, and industrial associations and enterprises as plan executants. It is not wholly adequate because some institutions with their own profit-and-loss balancing—the banks—are part of the central authorities, while others carried on the public accounts are executants— design offices and research institutes have often been in this category, though their status has varied.

Business accountability also draws a line at the level of the enterprise units within which they do not have balance sheets of their own, although various techniques of cost accounting (termed 'intra-enterprise accountability') are practised. The anomaly involved in the Hungarian 'large enterprise' (see page 44)—a merger wherein constituent enterprises retain their balance-sheets—may be resolved by classifying it as an industrial association.

The planning authorities include the political agencies with control over the economy, whether they are part of the government machinery or of the communist party, and have been termed by other writers the 'system's directors', the 'centre' or 'the central planning board'. They are, of course, concerned with all the functions of state, and in the present context may be seen as the economic executive of a combined party and government structure the nature of whose intimacy is a matter for political sociology. It is nevertheless necessary to discuss (pages 157–9) the group's heterogeneity in the various countries on the issue of reform.

4
Scope of Planning

THE POLITICAL philosophy of the communist parties of eastern Europe, as that of the Soviet Party, judges the political, economic and social acts of its citizens by their contribution to communal objectives, formulated—until an ideal state of 'self-administration' be reached—by democratic organs of government. All economic activities should hence be available for such common purposes. This view engendered the assumption underlying the directive system that a national plan should be universal, i.e. that as much as possible be brought within the perimeter of the plan. Nationalisation, and the incorporation of nearly all the remaining firms into co-operatives or entities with state participation (over both of which the planning authorities exercise a considerable measure of control), made such comprehensive planning feasible in industry, and Lenin's legacy of 'democratic centralism' as the mode of Party-life shaped its form: the socialist enterprise must operate according to a plan approved by a superior agency whose plan, in turn, is the aggregate of those of its subordinates. A plan should exist for every decision-making unit, but every unit takes part in plan construction.

The 'guided market' abandons both universality and centralism, though it is intendedly as much democratic and socialist as, conceptually, is the directive system. Advocates of the Czechoslovak and Hungarian reforms have been unanimous in stressing that plan and market are indissolubly related in their mechanism, and emphasise that 'without government planning no purposive development can be achieved and without market relations no rational allocations can be realised'. The plan still programmes the economy as a whole, but the market regulates many of the activities embraced in a directive plan and is, in turn, regulated by controls on prices and incomes.

Three steps may be distinguished in elaborating the directive plan, of which the first takes place within the central authorities, when broad guide-lines are formulated. The early priority, copying the example of the Soviet Union in the 'thirties, was industrialisation based upon rapid growth of producers' goods. Those countries with surplus population in agriculture (Bulgaria, Hungary, Poland and Rumania) saw manpower transfer as a major contributor to industrial growth and the more developed, with records of high pre-war unemployment, took industrial enterprises as job-creating: in Poland the process was caustically termed 'keeping unemployment behind the factory gate', and in Czechoslovakia, 'social employment'. The broad 'orientational' targets were hence based partly on demographic factors and upon the speed at which new enterprises could be set up and existing enterprises enlarged. The limit to this pace, in the absence of an inflow of foreign capital, was the volume of real domestic resources, of which those not reserved for personal and social consumption and the needs of government could be invested.

In the early years of planning in eastern Europe, the macro-economic balance exhibiting this division of national product was drawn up in only the sketchiest form, and the guide-lines were set out rather as desired additions to the previous year's production. Enterprises elaborated their plans according to those guide-lines and matched their targets for outputs with those for proposed inputs of current and capital resources. Consistency was, in principle, achieved at the operational level, and the aggregations of drafts by superior agencies provided the central authorities with a coherent plan. On the basis of this upward flow of information, the central authorities elaborated the final plans, verifying the consistency of inputs and outputs for selected physical goods through 'material balances', drafts of which had been used at the initial planning stage. The indicators of outputs and inputs and financial corollaries were then dispatched down the hierarchy as directive or informative plan indicators.

The universal character of planning and its consequential form of plan construction are still accepted in four countries, but the Czechoslovak and Hungarian reforms now limit the planning process to the first stage, namely, macro-planning at the central level, where the guide-lines issued by the planning authorities in Hungary are, and in Czechoslovakia are intended to be, in the form of general monetary and fiscal measures, with resort to direct controls and instructions only in the exceptional cases of defence and vital foreign trade interests. The term 'plan' for the annual document was replaced in Czechoslovakia in 1968 and 1969 by 'economic directives of the government', but was again used in 1970; it has been retained in Hungary, but in conjunction with a new text 'directives of credit policy'. Bulgaria, which retains substantial features of directive planning, has made a step in the same direction by issuing the annual plan as a combined financial and economic statement; Rumania, similarly, for the first time unified the drafting of the financial and production elements in its 1970 annual plan.

Under the guided market system the test for consistency which plays a major role in the second stage of directive planning is thus undertaken as part of a normal commercial appreciation by the enterprise or the industrial association; no need therefore arises for a third stage in which those plans are reported back and final directives are issued. In place of the two latter stages, the reporting of short-term indicators is required only in so far as deviations from the macro-economic plan can be corrected by the instruments at the disposal of the planning authorities. The frequency with which those instruments can be changed is peculiar to each, and, to that extent, the need for distinct plan periods ceases.

Plan periods

During the score or so years under central planning three periods of plan became standard: long-term projections of

15–20 years' duration ('perspective' plans), medium-range plans (usually for five years but occasionally for six or three), and short-run (annual or biennial) operational plans (or, under the guided market system, annual sets of policy-measures). Quarterly operational plans, although theoretically a break-down of the annual plan, became in practice those to which enterprises worked and, due to intervening changes by the central authorities, often did not sum to the year's programme originally handed down.

While medium-term annual plans are enacted into law, or adopted by congresses of communist parties, and thereby—at least in theory—bind the planning or Party authorities as the case may be, the perspective plan only sketches a desired development path. When they began to be drafted in the early 'sixties these were intended to facilitate medium-term planning by establishing a set of reference points with a longer time-horizon—they were by no means a comprehensive programme for all activities covered in the medium-term—and to attenuate 'discontinuous' planning. Five years had proved too short for the completion of some industrial objectives, and a tendency had become manifest for investment projects to be started in unison at the beginning of a plan period, and irrational efforts bent towards completing them in time for reporting on their fulfilment in the final year of the plan. Reports by the statistical office, as one of the central authorities, are normally issued at the end of each year and quinquennium. The need to report the degree of fulfilment led executants to a clustering of effort towards the end of each period for which the expenditure of resources and effort was quite disproportionate to results achieved.

Because the long-term perspective comprised few of the very many targets written into the medium-term plan, an alternative solution to discontinuity—'rolling plans'—was also considered at about the same date, though actually introduced (and then but briefly) only in the USSR. The horizon of a rolling plan moves forward annually, the previous targets being projected twelve months forward in the light of actual developments during the year elapsed and of any change in medium-term policy.

A crucial shortcoming of directive practice, contrary to official hopes and declarations, was the priority which annual programmes invariably enjoyed over five-year plans. Only marginal efforts are being made to redress this balance, e.g. in Poland the probable indicators for the following year are now being added to annual obligatory targets, a procedure not unlike that of the British Treasury where spending targets are drawn up for the year after the budgetary exercise. In Hungary, too, the expected policy for a year ahead is communicated to enterprises when the annual plan is approved. There and in Czechoslovakia the planning function is conceived primarily for the medium-term, within which short-term policy and adaptation are formulated. The technical procedures being used for the Hungarian Fourth Five-year Plan (1971–5)—a 'two-level model' in which plan variants are elaborated and confronted by detailed commodity groups at both the national and the branch level—are the most sophisticated in eastern Europe. To underscore the new importance of medium-range planning Hungarian five-year plans will henceforth be enacted by parliament as well as approved by a Party congress.

Annual plans under the directive system have tended to supersede work on medium and long-term plans also because they were highly time-consuming. It was normal for the annual plan to take five or six months in passing down and up the planning procedure described on page 66: as some of this was on occasion an overlap into the year planned, enterprises did not receive a firm set of targets until the year to which the targets applied was already a month or two old; cases of plans not being finally communicated to the enterprise until April of the planned year were not unknown. Once the annual plan had been made definite, amendments began to be introduced, and enterprises frequently complained that they could not operate in a stable environment because so many corrections to the annual plan were made during its course. Little opportunity was thereby afforded planning commissions to concentrate upon the thorough examination of a medium-term plan. Before they adopted electronic data-processing and mathematical short cuts to the manipulation of large magnitudes, their time and resources were too exiguous to analyse the variants which the longer time-scale allowed. During an annual plan, the existing stock of capital and the location and skill-composition of manpower must largely be taken as given, but during five, or still more fifteen years, new technology and investment, and demographic movement, regional migration and labour training will substantially adapt the structure of capital and manpower. The economic reforms came at a time when mathematical and data-processing techniques were becoming capable of handling the vast masses of information needed to set up and compare different economic projections. Still other procedures may be coming to hand for mastery of the problems of multiple choice in a dynamic economy, and are needed at a time when the countries with radical reform are freeing the planning authorities from the task of detailed annual planning and correction. But in all countries the distortion of the price system (see Chapter 6) inhibits measurement and comparison of the efficiency of plan variants.

Instructions and reports

However efficient is the use of resources laid down in the directives, it can be greater or less in their execution. The scope for accidental error and deliberate misinformation in the transmission of data and instructions has already been briefly noted (page 32) and to this reference is again made in Chapter 9 (page 141). More importantly, the enterprise is faced with more choices than can be resolved by direct administrative order from a superior organisation. For plan implementation, therefore, the planning authorities need a management mechanism both to conduce plan executants to fulfil the targets addressed to them, or to follow certain general policies, and to induce them to take decisions on matters not covered by such directives in a manner which would both increase efficiency and be compatible with the fulfilment of explicit targets.

The mechanism may be seen as a flow of information passing through a framework of external rules to act upon enterprise dispositions. Of these three constituents, it was for long only the flow which transmitted the information embodied in the annual plan; the framework of external rules and the internal dispositions were much less frequently changed; the reforms of the directive system embody some of the pressure on the enterprise in the two sets of regulations. The information incorporated in the first component of the mechanism works both ways, from the planning authorities to the executants and vice versa. The specific information carriers within it may be parametric—viz. constant relationships between enterprise activities, such as the price of its materials, the wage tariffs for its employees, the liability to tax or the rate of interest on its capital—or non-parametric—i.e. administrative orders. As already shown, the aim of the Bulgarian, and the practice of the Czechoslovak and Hungarian, reforms substitute market-parametric information for state-parametric; the move from non-parametric to parametric systems is government policy in the GDR, Poland and Rumania; even in Albania, hitherto non-parametric *par excellence*, the Director of the Institute of Economics (created in 1969) made the balance of 'supply and demand' the subject of one of his first public statements.

The rules outside the enterprise comprise the financial system (notably taxation and banking, with ancillary roles for insurance and foreign-exchange transaction) and the regulations governing the purchase of materials, the recruitment of labour and the disposal of output. The disposition may for the directive system be classified under four heads. First, the general accounting system for the enterprise, viz. the manner of constructing its balance sheet and the definition and classification of costs and assets; second, the 'success indicator(s)' for the enterprise—volume of profit, sales or revenue, or some relationship of these to costs or assets; third, rules for rewarding management, technicians and operatives in relation to the indicators (not all ranking equally nor all entitling to rewards), together with any sanctions imposed upon management, technicians or workers for failure to meet an indicator (demotion, dismissal or monetary fine); finally, the rules for the distribution of profits and depreciation charges between the enterprise, the industrial association and the planning authorities, and the restriction, if any, on the freedom of the enterprise to dispose of those funds thereby left to its discretion.

Under the guided market the indicator to which rewards are attached is enterprise revenue or profit, but its volume is not planned, and remuneration and investment funds are paid therefrom. The dispositions remaining concern the manner of constructing the balance sheet and the allocation of profit or revenue.

The regulations for enterprise accountancy are not considered further in this study. Appendix, Table V sets out (for the eastern Europe states, other than Albania, and for the USSR and Yugoslavia) the main heads under which the financial situation of the enterprise must be recorded according to regulations valid for 1968. As the Rumanian rules were radically revised that year, those operative in 1969 are also included; the Czechoslovak and Hungarian practices are as amended by changes introduced concurrently with the general economic reforms of 1967 and 1968 respectively. The translation of the headings is literal: an attempt to find terms closer to, say, British corporate accounting procedures might have induced misleading comparisons. Two features which stand out in relation to western practice are the absence of an entry for liabilities against assets—precluded by the nature of state ownership—and the discrete listing, instead of articulation, of financial flows—a legacy from the priority of statistical reporting over double-entry book-keeping.

The history of eastern Europe under central planning has demonstrated the strong interdependence between the role of central planning and the type of management mechanism. Whenever the character of central planning was at its most universal and detailed, a non-parametric management mechanism was employed. When, on the other hand, the government narrowed the scope of central planning and consequently set plan tasks in more general terms, the management mechanism became more parametric. Economic parameters can only be utilised for guiding plan executants, and if an exact implementation of detailed indicators is required, resort must be had to administrative orders. Failure to appreciate this has led to economic crisis, although the worst—that of Czechoslovakia in 1962–3—may be attributed to an accumulated macro-economic disequilibrium. Poland in 1957–8 and Czechoslovakia in 1958–60 permitted the firm wider autonomy under the management mechanism but without significantly diminishing the flow of directive information. Czechoslovakia went so far as to allow enterprises control over 55 per cent of investment funds, by allowing them to retain depreciation funds and a guaranteed share of profit—introducing the concept of stable 'normatives' which were later prominent in enterprises' demands for reform in the mid-sixties (page 134). Conversely, in the early years of central planning the flow of directive information flooded enterprises before they were told their internal dispositions or even furnished with external regulations. Until the latest round of reform, the tendency of the government, when faced with the economic consequences of incompatibility between the information system and either of the two frameworks, was to reverse those changes which had gone furthest towards devolution: 'creeping re-centralisation' followed bouts of well-intentioned reform.

The 'experimenting enterprise'

Of the same nature is the transfer of a sample of enterprises to a new management mechanism. Experiments have been conducted in advance of the enactment of generally applicable reforms, to test managers' and workers' reactions and to compare results with those continuing upon the standard system. The first seem to have been in Poland at the end of 1956, when 45 enterprises were granted authority to spend their own depreciation funds, to modify their production plans and to choose contractors for any approved investment, and in Hungary in 1959, when a few ministry administrations were converted into industrial associations ('trusts'). The latest uses have occurred in Rumania in 1967, for trying out in 71 enterprises a system whereby premia are based solely on profit-plan fulfilment and are extended to all employees; and in Albania in 1969 to test three variants for calculating labour productivity for purposes of plan assessment.

Although, as the examples indicate, experiments are relatively modest in their variations from the ruling directive practice, difficulties have arisen when decisions made under the experiment conflict with those in other enterprises. The contradiction is summarised in a frequently-repeated anecdote on road-accident prevention: a mission from an east European country visits Britain and associates its lower ratio of motor vehicles to accidents with factors connected with driving on the left; the mission returns to recommend that the most accident-prone group of vehicles, motor cycles, should experimentally drive on the left while the remainder of traffic continues on the right.

5
Formulating Targets

WHEREAS SOME of the reconstruction programmes for one, two or three years introduced in the late 'forties can be seen as a prototype of the guided market system, the first medium-term development plans were explicitly built on the Soviet model. Bulgaria and Czechoslovakia began in 1949, Hungary and Poland the following year and Albania, the GDR and Rumania in 1951; all save the Polish (six years) were for five years and four had the same horizon (1955) as the five-year plan of the USSR. Since the expiry of those plans both Albania and Poland have always had a quinquennial successor; nowhere else has continuity in medium-term programming been complete.

The Albania succession is nevertheless somewhat formal, because its five-year plans were fundamentally rewritten during their course. Its first (1951–5) was pared of a too zealous imitation of Stalin's programmes when the Soviet leader died; the second and third were changed at mid-point because the Soviet Union increased, and respectively withdrew, its development assistance; the fourth, drafted with belated inspiration from the Chinese 'Great Leap Forward' and overtaken by the 'Cultural Revolution', was adjusted in course to the eclipse of both concepts.

Bulgaria suspended its five-year plan in 1951 and resumed a five-year plan in 1953; a three-year plan was envisaged to carry its terminal year to alignment with other eastern European countries (1960) but, in the event, a five-year plan was introduced (1958–62) which was in turn suspended at the end of 1960; quinquennial plans have been enacted for the two following periods. Czechoslovakia, after terminating its first plan at the appointed date, did not introduce a new five-year plan until 1956; the successor to that plan (1961–5) was suspended in 1962 and no new medium-term plan was officially operative until 1966; this, nevertheless, had virtually no life at all, being overwhelmed by the wave of radical change in 1967. The GDR also completed its first five-year plan, but its second had only one year's validity and a seven-year plan did not follow it until 1959; this, however, ceased to be operative in 1962 and a new seven-year plan was delayed until 1964, thereby putting the country in the place of having the longest intermissions between plans in eastern Europe. Hungary had no medium-term plan to cover 1955, and the five-year plan which it began in 1956 was nullified by the work stoppages and the battle-damage during the suppression of the 1956 uprising; a three-year plan bridged the gap 1958–60 until a five-year plan was started in 1961. Rumania would have had as straightforward a record as Poland had not a change of policy (towards a diversification which led the country into conflicts with other members of Comecon in the early 'sixties) caused it to merge the last year of its 1956–60 plan with a six-year plan for 1960–5. In the exceptional conditions of administrative chaos under the Great Purge in the USSR no integrated plan was drafted for 1938, 1939 and 1940, but for the eastern European states annual programmes were always available.

When the medium-term plans began (as has already been indicated on page 26), the pre-eminence of communist parties at home and of the Soviet Union in foreign affairs readily led to their formulation with priority to the development of heavy industry. Domestic political conditions permitted both the limitation of other options in discussion of the plan draft and a mechanism of implementation which tolerated no legitimate deflection from the planners' preferences. The draft plan was not open to discussion by an informed public opinion, and parliamentary approval was a formality. Once enacted, it was ostensibly binding upon all state entities and officials concerned; even its components and results were masked in a wave of secrecy which interrupted the flow of official statistical abstracts in eastern Europe from 1949 to 1956. Consumer rationing was general throughout the currency of the first round of plans and control over the trade unions disarmed opposition at the enterprise level; both facilitated adoption of a policy which favoured a high rate of investment and defence-spending by depressing real wages and manipulating piece-rates to the advantage of management.

The broad lines of this economic strategy seem to have been accepted by governments from late 1948 onwards: one of the first signs was the inclusion of investment in defence-oriented industries in the revision of the Hungarian medium-term plan in April 1949. They were evident in the goals which five countries published during 1949–50, but the outbreak of the Korean War and the imposition by NATO powers of embargos or severe restrictions on sales to eastern Europe (covering about half of all items moving in international trade) led the Soviet Union to demand targets implying a higher rate of self-sufficiency in industry and greater spending on sectors with armament potential.

Comecon, newly founded, was not employed to elaborate a common plan strategy, for the USSR preferred to use communist party channels for communications of a broad nature, and its own nationals, installed in economic ministries as visiting experts, for indicating procedures and tactics. It was in this fashion that, in late 1950 at a remote Hungarian village, a delegate of the Soviet Communist Party informed officials of the east European parties that the five-year plan targets for heavy industry would have to be increased. Czechoslovakia, the GDR and Hungary announced the appropriate revisions to their plans in 1951, Bulgaria revised its targets but made no formal re-draft, and Poland issued higher targets for the relevant industries without re-statement of the overall plan. The plans of Albania and Rumania, appearing after the Soviet instructions had been given, concentrated upon projects in the appropriate producer-goods sectors. Albania, until 1948 under Yugoslav influence, had become of military interest in the USSR when Yugoslavia began to receive United States and British assistance in 1950;

it was equipped with a Soviet naval (chiefly submarine) base, and put into its plan a steel-works which quite properly never materialised.

Until the pressure was relaxed by the death of Stalin and the Korean Armistice, the medium-term plans were little more than bundles of directives on a few key industries. Priorities were adapted to give some temporary preference to the development of consumer goods in 1953-5 under the 'New Course' of the GDR and Hungary. The second round of medium-term plans was affected, as has already been indicated, by the political revolution in Hungary and Poland and by the partial economic reform in those countries and in Czechoslovakia. The third set, covering 1960-5, was characterised by an excessive concentration on long-maturing industrial projects which induced a serious attempt to co-ordinate plans through Comecon. Rumanian intransigence in 1962-4 and a new wave of economic reform, starting in 1964, demoted Comecon's role until the reassertion of Soviet political authority in August 1968 endowed it—by decisions of April 1969—with a co-ordinatory function. By then, the plans for 1966-7 had been disrupted by reforms in the two most trade-intensive members, Czechoslovakia and Hungary, and the new integration was scheduled for the plans to run from 1971 to 1975.

Macro-economic objectives

Such plan co-ordination, like the forming of any national plan, must take account of the production possibilities of the economy (including the gain from trade with other countries) and the preferences both of consumers and of the planning authorities. Such production possibilities (including the international terms of trade) and consumers' preference are constraints from the viewpoint of the planners, and their importance is inversely proportional to the distance of the plan horizon. Substantial changes in the structure of production or consumption can take place only after an adequate lapse of time, and the goals of any medium-term plan are a

60

compromise between the planning authorities' preference and the constraints of resources and consumers.

The underlying objectives conceived by the authorities (ultimately the leaders of the communist parties), which could, say, include economic independence from, or complementarity to the USSR, military strength or a better standard of living, might be discernible in the perspective plans, but they are, however, too few and insufficiently detailed to bear much examination. The most that can be seen of the priority scales which the planning authorities embrace is in the fulfilment pattern of medium-term plans, which are a mixture of desired long-range ends and short-run choice among scarce means.

During the 'fifties, and even subsequently, targets for the consumption sector were the regular victim when goals for capital and defence goods were put in jeopardy. Because capital formation was—for reasons set out in this and the next chapter—planned to be greater than construction and equipment availabilities, *ad hoc* re-arrangements were made of the medium-term plans (and often of annual plans) in which those responsible in the central authorities for non-productive projects (especially housing) and consumer-goods branches argued in vain for the maintenance of their appropriations. The Polish experience of plans for the increase in real wages (money wages adjusted for changes in the cost of living) may be cited as an example. An increase of 40 per cent was laid down in the plan for 1950–5; the official report on fulfilment claimed that an increase of 27 per cent was achieved but it was virtually admitted at the Central Committee meeting of the Polish Workers' Party, following the election of Gomulka to its First Secretaryship in October 1956, that this claim was spurious; a revised figure—a 4 per cent rise for 1950–5 —was published twelve years later.

In the subsequent plan, 1956–60, a 30 per cent increment was sought but the actual rise of 29 per cent had little claim to have been planned, because a 20 per cent rise took place during the first two years and there was a 2 per cent decline in real wages in the terminal year. In the 1961–5 plan a 23 per cent increment was intended, but only an 8 per cent gain was achieved.

Targets for personal and social consumption, of which those for real wages are a part, are in the last resort the only objectives which can be written into a perspective plan. Investment is required, not for its own sake, but for the flow of consumption which it will eventually yield. The increase in consumption is accompanied by changes in its composition both because the pattern of consumers' expenditure alters with income and because the relative production costs of consumers' goods and services vary with the aggregate volume of expenditure. The perspective plan is hence essentially a derivative of the planners' assessment of the growth rate which is feasible and the desired pattern of consumption; these are inter-related because, on the one hand, the feasible growth rate depends on the desired structure of output, and, on the other hand, the composition of consumption depends upon the final size of consumer expenditure.

Because planned rates of growth are high, the appropriate pattern of consumption should in principle be that of the consumers with correspondingly high incomes at present (allowance being made for changes in relative costs of production and for the introduction of new products and substitutes for existing goods and services). Production for the consumer in eastern Europe, however, has largely been geared to the needs of the average earner. Those with incomes much above the mean have been unable, in the absence of consumer sovereignty, to evoke the production of the goods and services on which they would wish to spend; the structure of their outlay is clearly not that which would be selected by the planners when that higher income became the average. Households with high incomes thus buy more food and drink and fewer cars, housing and tourism than they prefer. In the absence of domestic expenditure patterns usable for a high-income plan, reliance is placed upon 'scientifically-determined norms', a combination of expert assessments of desirable compositions of diet, housing and leisure-use and of consumer research through questionnaires, and experience in capitalist market economies.

While such methods are only partial guides to consumer behaviour at future and higher levels of income, the central authorities have it in their power to influence consumer expenditure towards the pattern thus established by their control over retail prices, imports and advertising. Under the directive system, eastern Europe represents for consumers' goods a marketing executive's ideal, to the extent that the optimum scale of production may be chosen and consumer demand tailored by price, domestic monopoly power and advertising to match that output. Use of the guided market model does not change the need for long-run prognoses of consumption: they become, rather, forecasts which, while still using the concept of norm, are closer to those undertaken by large capitalist concerns. Czechoslovakia is certainly the most advanced in consumption forecasting, in work developed at the Research Institute for Trade, at the Planning Research Institute and in the Office of the Prime Minister in Prague and at the Institute for Research into Living Standards in Bratislava.

Under either system the role of the planning authorities in establishing a perspective plan is to choose from among different consumption patterns, as exhibited by any of the modes of calculation, that which can be produced with different mixtures of available resources. Under directive practice, considerations of efficiency are mainly limited to selection of the way to achieve stated goals, rather than in selecting among series of objectives.

At the beginning of the 'sixties, and in line with the Soviet Communist Party's Programme covering the years to 1980, Bulgaria, the GDR, Hungary and Rumania drew up perspective plans for the same span. A draft fifteen-year plan prepared for Poland by the distinguished economist, Kalecki, then Director of Perspective Plans at the State Planning Commission, was, of all, the most internally consistent and methodologically novel. It was, however, rejected by the Government which promulgated only a few isolated targets for 1980. Czechoslovakia, at that time in a crisis of its medium-term plan, similarly stated only a few goals, not woven together into a comprehensive programme. In 1966 a ten-year plan (1966–75) for the energy sector was approved in Rumania.

The perspective plan is the product of a special department, institute or *ad hoc* committee of the planning commission, helped as necessary by other departments and ministries. Since such long-term targets (which may be approved as 'Directives' of a Communist Party Congress) have no binding force, ministries—and still less enterprises—are not overly concerned to influence goals in their own favour. Short- and medium-term plans, on the other hand, intimately affect their operation under the directive system, and, even if not so required, they would try to interpose their views in the drafting process within the central authorities.

Macro-economic aims are determined at the highest political level (Party Central Committee and Council of Ministers), those for an annual plan in principle incorporating the relevant progressions from the medium-term plan, with adjustment for actual trends: they are of the nature of the share of investment and consumption in national income, the rate of growth of industrial production or wage increments for particular industries in relation to their expected productivity. The extent to which the annual plan respects the implications of the medium-run targets obviously varies with current circumstances and the precision with which the latter were drafted: Poland and Rumania have attached particular importance to setting out five- (or six-) year programmes in annual segments. Rumania is going as far as confirming five-year plans, each with annual goals, for every major enterprise in 1971–5, but it is hard to see how so detailed a set of targets could survive any macro-economic revision while the plan was being implemented.

The Rumanian procedure is at the further extreme from

64

Hungarian practice since 1968. The five-year plan will become the chief instrument of planning, and more targets will be written into it than into the annual programme, although neither will be broken down for any enterprise: goals will be at most specified by the industrial branch. The perspective plan will form broad, but not detailed, guidance for three quinquennia. As is shown below (page 122), great importance is attached in the Hungarian reform to the assurance of a stable environment for the individual enterprise.

'Breaking down' the plan

The normal practice under the directive system is for ministries and associations to draft annual and quarterly plans to the enterprise. The aggregation of replies is accompanied at each stage by negotiations to achieve balance between targets and capabilities, that is, to assure that the partial sectoral plans under consideration are practicable and are consistent with others in the same administration. Attempts have been made to stimulate 'planning from below', viz. to transform enterprises from adopters of a central draft to initiators of independently-conceived proposals. A notable example was the 'counter-plan' (*protiplan*) in Czechoslovakia in 1950–1952, but the sole example in current use is that of Poland introduced in 1968, both for annual plans (starting with 1970) and for the 1971–5 medium-term directives: the State Planning Commission makes known some guide-lines to which industrial associations should seek to conform in drawing up proposals and uses them as criteria when it receives replies. Habituated to much fuller directives, and knowing that the Commission decides in the last resort, associations have not found the new procedures easy. Contributors to a symposium of August 1969 reported that associations were hindered by inadequate information on projected demand (especially from abroad) and on the technical processes for which equipment and foreign-exchange could be made available. If, as there are grounds for believing, the new procedure foreshadows greater autonomy for the association by 1971, the planned structure for the quinquennium then beginning could furnish the information and stability within which better decentralised decisions could be taken. Difficulties have been exaggerated by the concurrent review of wholesale prices, the results of which (see page 90) are not available to enterprises for drafting their plans. Although it is the government's intention to attach much weight to associations' proposals when the Plan is being finalised, many of their projected outputs may prove to be less profitable at the new, than at current, prices. In Rumania, from 1970, industrial ministries took over from the Planning Committee authority to 'break down the plan', but in the longer run it is hard to see a better solution than to eliminate the procedure, as in Hungary now.

For the typical directive economy one downward and one upward movement in the hierarchy are in theory sufficient, but in practice the steps are repeated many times at each level with negotiation and decision successively approximating the components to a consistent overall plan. The magnitude of the task involved and the obstacles to virtually simultaneous negotiation with all parties in any exchange (or their simulation by electronic computation) prevent all the consequences and interrelationships of changes introduced in this process from being taken into account. For this and other reasons (described later in this chapter, pages 73–6) the final plan (as approved successively by the Politburo of the Communist Party, the Council of Ministers and National Assembly) is never fully consistent: unexpected disequilibria invariably arise during the execution of the plan. In consequence most of the efforts of the planners have been devoted to bringing requirements and availabilities into short-term equilibrium. The technique of input–output tabulation (a record of the sectors making and the sectors taking delivery of goods and services during a year) has been used everywhere save in Rumania (where a decision of 1961 to compose one was apparently revoked and not again taken until 1967, for completion in 1970) and Albania. Input-output can verify the consistency of planned production and utilisation of groups of products, but not of the many thousands of individual goods and services which operational plans regulate.

Drafting the inter-industry relationships and other technologies which relate current inputs to output and present investment to future production differs in Czechoslovakia and Hungary by being confined to the central authorities, including the industrial board or ministries and new inter-ministerial agencies, the Board for Technology and Investment and the National Board for Technical Development respectively. The outcome, called in Hungary a synthetic balance (of some two hundred products), shows where tensions and surpluses are likely to occur, but is not of course used for directives to enterprises. By contrast, the majority continue to employ the Soviet 'method of successive approximations'. Better described as administrative iteration, this requires the negotiation of provisional entries as inputs or outputs in material balances targets within and between government departments and between them and industrial associations until a feasible set emerges which conforms to the specified macro-economic objectives.

Reform of the directive system has invariably included an attempt to make the annual operational plan more manageable by reducing its scope and delegating negotiations to industrial associations and enterprises. Trimming the number of indicators handed down to the enterprise was particularly important in Hungary in 1954 (though a new rise began in 1956) and in Poland and Rumania in 1956. In the latter the number of industrial targets, 900 in 1955, had reached 1000 in 1956, but was cut in the 1957 Plan to 700. At the same time a version of the 'counter-plan' was abandoned (see p. 65)— Hungary being the pioneer in 1954—that the enterprise should demonstrate its ideological enthusiasm by volunteering higher indicators than those drafted by the central authorities. The reduction in direct instructions was often illusory, for the 'eliminated' indicators continued to be set up, but not—in the words of an Hungarian official in 1955—'in writing ...

because we did not want to run the risk of being charged with widening the field of approved plan indicators'. Even today the formal number of plan indicators is supplemented by administrative orders—counting as such only those orders the non-fulfilment of which evokes a financial penalty: in Poland there are some 80 administrative orders among the 120–140 targets applicable to the enterprise.

By that time the severest period of shortages had passed: with Stalin's death and the relaxation of the NATO embargo, there was less pressure to invest in heavy industry and defence, and the opportunity arose to narrow the scope of producer-goods rationing; only Poland and Hungary made serious inroads at the time, Poland reducing the number of centrally-allocated items from 1575 in 1955 to 1088 in 1957 and 455 in 1958, and Czechoslovakia made a modest cut in 1958 when some decentralisation was abortively attempted (see page 55). In other countries significant change had to await the decision to engage in broader reform. When Bulgaria made its first round of change, the number of such goods was reduced from 1060 in 1965 to 164 in 1966; by 1966 Czechoslovakia had reduced its total to 76, when Hungary still had nearly 400 under allocation, cut by 1968 to less than 50 (mainly raw materials, for which a rise to equilibrium price had not been authorised), and thereby leaving 'material-technical supply' almost wholly to the market mechanism.

The allocations were effected by the Ministry of Planning in Czechoslovakia and by the Board of Prices and Materials in Hungary. In addition industrial associations continued to ration certain other goods among their members in Czechoslovakia, either as consumers or as suppliers. Since Hungarian ministries issue no directives to enterprises or their associations (although, it may be reiterated, they still retained the legal right to do so), the plans for individual commodity-groups elaborated in the National Planning Office are only projections, but in 1968, the first year of market-relationships between enterprises, the actual pattern of production by sector was said to be closer to that envisaged by the central planning authorities than in any previous year when directives had been the rule. The industrial ministry can express desires that certain goods be manufactured in a given quantity, but if such a course involves the enterprise in any financial loss, the ministry should provide due compensation; such wishes on the part of a Ministry are expected to arise only in connection with the commitments for the armed forces and for export to Comecon members under long-run agreements etc. In 1968 Hungarian enterprises in fact needed no pressing to fulfil export programmes to such countries, for sales there were easier to secure than markets in the West.

In the first half of 1968 the Czechoslovak Government was following the same path, but twelve months later directives were again being transmitted downward 'by agreement'— from the Ministry of Planning and the Board for Industry to associations and to certain large enterprises. Such agreements, introduced during the second half of 1969, were concluded to assure either the output of certain 'key' consumers' goods (to counter inflationary pressure) or the export of products to Comecon partners. The agreements provide for fines if the target production or delivery is not fulfilled.

On the other hand, financial autonomy was strengthened by regulations, taking effect in 1970, whereby enterprises are endowed with their own working capital. The financial dispositions described in Chapter 8 remain valid and the country should not cease to be called a guided market economy until the enterprise loses its authority as a profit centre.

The 'inter-enterprise agreement system', introduced as a definitive stage of economic reform in January 1969, is the Bulgarian version of the guided market. Two sets of draft plans (annual and, for 1971–5, quinquennial) are established, one by the central authorities, the other by associations and enterprises. The latter are, unlike the new Polish system (page 65), informed in detail of the former's draft, but are not bound to adhere to it in their text; final choice of the plan targets lies with the central authorities, but the influence upon them of the associations is considerable. In drawing up drafts, an enterprise keeps in contact with the drafting being done by its suppliers and customers and its final plan is established as a set of contracts with them. These elaborate rather than supersede obligatory indicators, of which, from 1969, seven remain (see page 106), and are seen as the principal instrument of micro-economic co-ordination. The contracts cover prices, qualities and delivery dates (penalties for non-fulfilment of which may go up to 5 per cent of the value of the goods involved).

The system of balances

Irrespective of their use in instructing enterprises and associations, 'balances' have not lost their utility for assessing macro-economic equilibrium. It has already been observed that those denominated in physical units ('material balances') are retained under the guided market to identify shortages and elsewhere serve as the basis for commodity rationing. As their name implies, one set of entries shows the total availability (from domestic production, imports and running down stocks), the other sets out aggregate demand (for intermediate use, current consumption, investment, export and augmenting stocks), and the 'balancing method' co-ordinates the two in time and space, ensuring also that any priorities are executed wherever the power to issue directives permits it.

Classified by scope, a material balance is either termed 'economic' (i.e. it covers commodities which are not necessarily centrally allocated and serves solely to verify the coherence of plan targets), or 'users' (for allocated products and in which the demand side specifies the principal non-retail users of the given product, compiled if necessary by region). The Hungarian usage for 'economic balance' is 'synthetic', but the adjective is commonly used elsewhere in east Europe to mean 'combined'—(see pages 36 and 105).

Where these balances are still used as the basis for directives, the recent reforms have not only, as just observed, diminished the number of balances but also simplified their administration. The decree of October 1965 introducing the second round of reform in Poland limited approval by the Council of Ministers to the balances dealing with thirteen products (specified types of coal and steel, aluminium, zinc, copper, lead, cement, timber, meat and food grain); it restricted ratification of a balance by the State Planning Commission to approximately 80 items; and it left the remainder of goods not on free sale to enterprises to be allocated at the discretion of ministers and directors. In order to secure maximum conformity to the planned distribution, some products are still designated as subject to 'use control', whereby the supplier is required to check that the delivery is utilised by the consumer in the way specified in the underlying balance and its supporting regulations; an enterprise manager diverting such supply to an unauthorised use is liable to a maximum of three years' imprisonment.

By their nature, material balances cannot be the sole instrument of an operational plan because the units in which they are compiled are different, and if converted into values by the application of some aggregative price (see page 77), their totals do not sum to the entire production of any industry since numerous items are not covered by any material balance.

From the first, therefore, the central authorities have employed parallel financial balances capable of separation into (and verification of) the accounts of enterprises and their relations with households. Neither two decades of application of Soviet-type financial balances in eastern Europe, nor the longer experience in their country of origin, have resulted in procedures which enable short-term money transactions to be identified with physical flows with sufficient precision. This deficiency—manifested in inflationary pressure—has been one of the chief factors in demoting physical planning under the reforms.

The two macro-economic fields covered by financial planning are the relations between households and state and co-operative enterprises (the 'balance of money income and expenditure of the population') and the flows within the public sector (the 'financial plan of the state'): examples are shown in Tables I–III in the Appendix (pages 166–8). They have been employed, in broadly the same form, since the first medium-term plans, except in Albania where they appeared in 1959.

The form of the national plan as it emerges from these balances comprises a massive volume of documentation in four of the countries where directives are still the rule; Albania has made little use of macro-economic financial balances. The plan for each branch of industry is categorised by ministry and by industrial association, and includes targets in physical and value terms (in an annual plan in constant and current prices, in a medium-term plan in constant prices) and a set of 'technical-economic indicators' which substantiate the plan (the more detail being given in an annual than a medium-term plan). Examples of such indicators are productivity per worker, material inputs per unit of output, stoppages as a percentage of the work-day (the expected halts being due, e.g. to repair work or failure to receive materials, and not, for a plan, at least, to strikes), the average weight per unit of specified products, the proportion of high-quality items in total output and the share of manual work in total non-administrative labour time.

The plans for other branches of the economy (conventionally grouped into agriculture, construction, transport, foreign and domestic trade) tend to be somewhat less complex. The implications of each of these sectoral plans are considered together in a group of functional plans, i.e. material and technical supplies, investment, employment and wages, and production costs. The plan document also includes certain projections imputed from the financial balances, such as increments in real wages or in the real income of collective farmers, and some calculations which derive not from any balance but from special projections, notably the growth of net material product (the national income, excluding certain services defined as 'non-productive'); none of these eventuate in obligatory indicators, because no such target can be broken down into orders to an individual unit ('addressed', in the term borrowed from Soviet usage).

The guided market economy does not require a form of financial planning capable of being broken down in this way. The Czechoslovak authorities are undertaking research into the practical uses to which fully-articulated national accounts can be put. The Commission for Statistics has established a special unit, and other work is in progress at the Research Institute of the Ministry of Finance, at the State Bank and in the Ministry of Planning. In Hungary variants for 1975 were compared in the 'two-level' model (see page 51), covering output, imports and exports, of 490 products (classed as made with existing, reconstructed or new capacity). Resource use is projected under manpower, gross investment (separated into construction and domestic and imported machinery), the wage-bill and the balance of trade.

Accuracy of projection

Because the reform schemes of those two countries rejected the use of plan indicators for enterprises, they set aside the assumption of the central authorities—once as widespread in east Europe as it still is in the USSR—that an over-fulfilment was to be preferred to an under-fulfilment or a precise accomplishment of a goal. The more recent view is that any deviation, whether positive or negative, from a plan the targets of which are consistent is unwelcome.

Projection has been particularly difficult in sectors where it depended at least partly on the decisions of private individuals. Thus the employment plan for the socialised sector in Poland was one-third over-fulfilled in the three-year plan (1946–9), and the five-year plan (1955–60), and two-thirds over-fulfilled in the five-year plan (1961–5); the 40 per cent under-fulfilment in the six-year plan (1950–5) arose only because the target included the expected number of collective farmers in the abortive collectivisation drive. Wage payments were 34 per cent in excess of plan in 1955–60 and 115 per cent in excess in 1961–5; the planned value of the wage-bill is set by the central authorities, but they cannot assure that individuals will apply for the places provided, or that the wages offered will be judged acceptable: enterprise managers edge earnings upward in order to recruit and keep staff for which the planned wage is not an equilibrium one.

An example of over-fulfilment due to inconsistency in the plan can be drawn from the level of industrial inventories. In the nine years following the first Polish reform of 1956, the planned volume was in two years more than three times exceeded, in three years exceeded by two-and-a-half times and in the remaining four years exceeded by percentages varying between 19 and 59 per cent. There are, indeed, even traces of the old priorities whereby the output of producers' goods was a more favoured candidate for overfulfilment than of consumers' goods: the Polish Five-year Plan for 1966–70 maintained the traditional relationship between producers' and consumers' goods by laying down targets of a 48 per cent increment in the one, against a 37 per cent increment in the other, but the likely fulfilment of those targets is that the producer-goods goal will be over-fulfilled by 15 per cent; but that for consumers' good under-fulfilled by 10 per cent.

Three factors may be relevant to the degree of accuracy of forecasts. Firstly, the economies have all shown such rapid industrial growth that the complexity of planning and the sheer volume of plan targets have increased as quickly, or perhaps even more quickly, than any benefits of greater experience, a more competent planning staff and improved computing equipment. Although the official index-numbers of global industrial production are subject to considerable reservations when compared with those of other countries, the increments they show between 1950 and 1967 give some idea of the magnitude involved: in Albania output was registered as rising 10·6 times, in Bulgaria 8·8 times, in Czechoslovakia 4·1 times, in the GDR 4·5 times, in Poland 5·6 times, in Hungary 4·5 times and in Rumania 8·4 times.

'Taut' planning has been a second consideration making for divergence from plan, the practice, that is, of planning output close to the ceiling of fixed capacity, working stocks, current supplies and foreign-exchange availabilities. Setting a target for an enterprise with minimum feasible slack was intended to offset its 'concealment of reserves' (that is, to assure itself leeway for the completion of tasks imposed by superior authorities); a 'taut' plan is also a legacy of the attitude to plan fulfilment as an 'heroic', quasi-military duty, born of the Soviet First Five-year Plan and nurtured in east Europe during the Cold War.

The tightening of inputs in relation to outputs had two principal effects on planning: distortions and divergences in plan fulfilment were magnified because the effects of any error could not be absorbed, and plan executants, at the second phase of compiling a plan, tended to report inaccurate statistics in order to insure themselves against the risk of subsequent under-fulfilment of the output plan; alternatively they dissimulated input needs: while no charge was being levied on fixed assets installed, enterprises sought to better their capital allocations by undervaluing the cost of investing in their plan (actual investment costs tended in Poland to be around one-quarter or one-third above planned outlay). In capital as in current inputs demands were pitched unrealistically high and output projections were made guardedly low: the technical coefficients of a material balance were *ab initio* faulty. This feature has its parallel in private corporations seeking government contracts in western countries. A study of United States weapons-programme contracts published in 1964 shows that average over-spending was no less than 2·2 times, and observes that 'firms submit excessively optimistic predictions of the proposed programme's quality, time and cost outcome ... (Lest the government agency) be shocked out of supporting a programme whose true costs were revealed at the outset ... they sought to disclose cost increases only gradually, after programmes had gained momentum and cancellations were difficult'.

75

Capital was in effect free for both investor (the central authorities) and the recipient (the enterprise) and it was by and large assumed that in each succeeding five-year plan an enterprise should be allowed more investment, in reflection of the dynamism desired for the entire economy. The inadequacy of construction facilities and equipment supply (aggravated in the latter case by sharp swings in the net import of machinery) resulted in a lengthening of average building times, the interruption of site works or installation and a consequent rise in the proportion of unfinished projects to total investment; it was countered by the *ad hoc* capital plan revisions already mentioned.

The third factor which has made it difficult to improve techniques of central planning has been the difficulty, experienced in virtually any civil service, of changing the organisation and methods of established personnel. It has already been observed that large-scale recruitment of the staff of the central authorities was undertaken at a time when political conformity was at a premium, and intellectual inventiveness at a discount. It may for that reason have seemed easier to devolve planning tasks than to alter the set ways of the central authorities: the outright replacement by the Soviet Government in 1957 of industrial ministries in Moscow by 105 regional authorities may be partly attributed to this consideration. Decentralisation of decision-making to industrial associations and enterprises, and even the acceptance of a constraint on the central authorities by a market, may in some measure be a consequence of the conservative position taken by the planners.

6
Prices

PRICES UNDER the directive system can be classified into those used for plan construction and those for plan implementation. Of the five prices used for industrial management, two types are employed in the first and three in the second category; those applicable to agriculture—including those for the procurement by state agencies of produce for delivery to processing factories—fall outside the scope of this study.

Plan-building prices

Of prices used for plan construction, aggregative prices are used for setting up a feasible and consistent plan. In any plan for production or consumption, different products or varieties of nearly homogeneous goods have to be summed; technological units (calories, horsepower, etc) are used for some planning purposes but have narrower spheres of application. Large aggregates—product groups for which no common technical measure is available—have to be employed in planning because the authorities have a limited capacity to handle information in disparate units: the use of electronic computers extends the limits within which the planning authorities can handle information and process its data into planning decisions; it does not eliminate them.

Aggregate prices are operational and consumer prices of a given date, the subsequent changes in which are not reflected in aggregate prices for the period of a medium-term plan. Supplemented by certain technological units, they figure in most plan calculations, without thereby playing an active role in planning choice: allocative decisions are reached by the process described in the preceding chapter.

The composition of a plan by determining goals for confrontation with resources lends itself to use of the programming prices mathematically implicit in its relationships. These, the duals of a linear programming problem, became acceptable to the Soviet planning authorities in the early 'sixties (where the concept of price was avoided by the term 'objectively-determined valuations') and had their first eastern European application in the GDR, Hungary and Poland. Bulgarian, Czechoslovak and Rumanian developments followed soon afterwards and, last in this line, the Albanian State Planning Commission jointly convened a conference on the subject with Tirana University in 1969.

Certainly the most significant use of programming to determine plan prices was made in Czechoslovakia in 1965–6, in preparation for the price reform of January 1967. To programme all wholesale prices prevailing in an economy as complex as the Czechoslovak would—according to the estimates of the pricing committee—have taken until 1970: a short cut was found whereby products were combined into 416 groups. This was few enough for a programming solution to be made parallel to the separate construction of prices on a 'two-channel model' (see page 87), both being used to draw up the new prices. The ratio of the new prices for a product group to the average of existing prices was applied to the prevailing price of each individual item, so that a full list of new prices could be issued. In the event the prices did not play their role in the overall economic reform, because enterprises—seeking to protect their profits against the introduction of market relationships—put in exaggerated cost estimates to the pricing committee: whereas the latter, from preliminary investigations, had expected that the programmed prices would exceed those prevailing by 19 per cent, the actual increment which emerged was 30 per cent. The reform was frustrated to the extent that enterprises had more profits at their disposal than the central authorities had intended: the new thrust of competition was blunted and the authorities had to go back on their undertaking not to raise business taxes and other government charges for an initial period.

The corresponding Hungarian price reform of January 1968 was wholly on the 'production price' model (see page

87), but programming is envisaged to derive expected price trends from the targets and forecasts of a medium-term plan. 'Shadow prices', those which the achievement of a specific objective requires in given conditions, have been frequently used in calculations of investment of foreign-trade efficiency. Within this group of prices are comprised also those implicit in cost/benefit calculations whereby the advantages to be derived from a project operative over a long period are reduced to a discounted value at the present time, for comparison with the cost involved.

Wholesale prices

Among the operational prices used for plan implementation under the directive system, wholesale prices have three functions. First, they carry the information to enterprises on supply and demand conditions and on the preferences of the planning authorities. Second, they constitute the measure whereby incentives are given for the execution of plans for profit (or profit-revenue ratios or gross revenue). Third, they are used to redistribute resources between enterprises and from enterprises as a whole to other expenditure determined by the government. The prices ruling for an external transaction converted at an appropriate multiple of the official exchange-rate may be used by domestic units as operational prices, as in the Hungarian wholesale price lists of 1959 and 1968. The 'multiplier', varying by commodity group in the first list but uniform in the second, expressed the input needed for obtaining by exports a unit of foreign exchange. Where the multiplier does not align the prices of internationally-traded goods to domestic levels, the differential—for which the GDR usage, *Preisausgleich*, has become standard —between a price so calculated and the domestic operational price is taken by the specialised foreign-trade corporation, and either taxed into, or subsidised by, the Ministry of Foreign Trade. Because all official rates are overvalued, imports yield a profit and exports make a loss, the net aggregate forming the *Preisausgleich*.

State enterprises are in most countries exempt from customs duties (which thus bear almost solely on personal imports), but since 1961 both Hungary and Bulgaria have established tariffs payable by the user, whether public or private. The Hungarian tariff was low until 1967 and the Bulgarian was not in practice levied, but in 1968 in the former and in 1969 in the latter, duties took the brunt of domestic protection. The so-called 'ideal prices' (see previous page) of the 1968 Hungarian reform were adjusted to actual prices partly under the influence of the pattern of foreign-trade prices.

Retail prices

The two other plan-implementation prices, retail prices and wages, are intended to execute the consumption plan—to ensure that the consumers' goods and services produced are sold for the total sum of wages (less savings and taxes) made available during the plan period. To ensure that the available supplies are taken, consumer-goods prices (including turnover tax or subsidy) are set at a level which will just clear the market; they should influence the pattern of household purchases in such a manner that the entire output of each product or service is disposed of (save when retail inventories are planned to increase). Households are thereby given freedom of choice among the products available, and are led by price relationships to choose the pattern desired by the planning authorities. The right of consumers to select their purchases is to be contrasted with the rationing which prevailed in the early post-war years, but it is not 'consumer's sovereignty', whereby household outlay significantly determines the structure of consumer-goods output.

If every retail commodity and consumer service forecast for production in the plan were to be sold, conditions of either repressed inflation or perfect planning would prevail. The first has never been absent from post-war eastern Europe and the second never attained. By setting consumer prices too low in relation to purchasing power and the planned volume of goods and services for consumption, the central authorities ensured that virtually everything supplied would be purchased. Inevitably there were too few goods and services to meet the demand, and queues and frustration were the norm. An inquiry in Hungary in the mid-fifties showed that the majority of shoppers, on being told that the item for which they asked was not available, purchased something different before leaving the shop. After one, or in some countries two, rounds of monetary confiscations, consumers were little willing to hold money in the expectation of buying later. In that first post-war decade almost everything that was for sale was snapped up, but as personal incomes rose and as confidence in the domestic currency (and in the stability of the regime) increased, households held off buying when the pattern of supplies and of prices did not meet their preferences. Thereafter, the volume of retail inventories increased: despite cut-price disposals for goods of particularly low quality and the introduction of deferred-payment terms (around 1958–9 in nearly all countries) for high-price durables, unsaleable stocks continued to accumulate.

The central authorities had three possible solutions consistent with maximising consumer welfare: they could adjust aggregate wages to total retail availabilities; they could bring the level of retail prices for planned turnover into line with aggregate wages; or they could change the ratios of retail prices to each other in closer conformity to the demand for individual goods and services at the given level and composition of household income. As is shown below (p. 84), they found after their first five-year plans that the size and composition of the wage-bill was virtually inflexible outside the annual increments allowable from productivity gains (or pressed out by 'wage drift'). That rigidity also barred the second path of adjustment, that of retail prices. Although they could at any time vary turnover tax (or the rate of profit in the consumer-goods industries), the central authorities were confronted with opposition by makers and implementers of retailing plans (who preferred constant prices as measures of the fulfilment of turnover) and by consumers (who had become habituated to a stable level and relationship of shop prices). An incidental consequence of the wane in shoppers' curiosity—the flair for seeking out 'the best buy' —may well have been a diminution of business acumen, primarily among those concerned with retail trade, but affecting also the general environment of the state entrepreneur. The shopper could compare prices and bargain only on the small free markets for private farm produce (from homestead plots in co-operative and state farms) and for second-hand and surplus-stock discount sales of consumers' durables; the field is much wider in the GDR (where 12 per cent of retail turnover remains in private hands), Hungary (where one retail shop in ten is privately owned), and Poland (where, from 1957 to 1967, 87 to 90 per cent of farm production has come from independent peasants); it is narrowest in Czechoslovakia (where industrialisation has eclipsed the farmers' market, and the last private shop was shut down in 1961).

The third way of using retail prices for plan implementation—their more accurate patterning to the demand for individual goods and services—has only recently been seriously followed. Czechoslovakia seems to have been the first to project how expenditure on specific items would alter with a change in price (price elasticity) or when wages rose (income elasticity). Few of the fruits of market research could, however, be gathered while retail prices were largely inflexible, and in practice adjustments have mainly been made on the supply side, i.e. allocating more goods of which there were too few at the constant prices and less when there were too many.

Where cost elasticity precluded expansion to the indicated output, the central authorities were all too ready to tolerate queues and dissatisfied customers. As a partial offset, an international barter grew up between the retail co-operatives of eastern Europe (and with that of the USSR) of those of their products which happened to be in surplus at the too-rigid domestic price. This trade was expected considerably to expand after Comecon's liberalisation of consumers' goods in 1969. Czechoslovakia increased imports of consumers' goods from capitalist countries when economic reform began, and authorised home enterprises to raise prices to those of the imported equivalent if quality and performance were identical.

Wages

Wages, the fifth and last group of price, are the main vehicle, as just stated, for distributing the planned consumers' dividend of the national product, and also for relating the manpower on offer to the planned employment. At the very outset of the directive system wages were thoroughly revised to a structure consonant with plan objectives: in essence, jobs were classified by skill and training, and enterprises were grouped by industrial branch, wherein the base-line wage (on which the standard skill-graduation was built) was ranked by plan priority. There is explicitly no comparability by occupation, a situation facilitated by the regrouping of craft unions into an industrial alignment.

The Rumanian wage system, introduced in 1949, may serve as an example. Each industry was given a base wage to which co-efficients—from 1 to 2·5—were applied corresponding to the eight skill categories; three further co-efficients were applied relating to the size, importance and degree of technical equipment of the enterprise and certain special supplements could be made for underground or particularly disagreeable work (or for individual regions in the case of mining and rail transport). The branch groups for calculating wages of technical staff were fewer than for operatives, but there were more co-efficients relating to size of enterprise (within which were three grades of section) and established on the basis of the number of operatives and of the value of fixed assets and of output. Where—as in the majority of cases —piece-rates were paid, the norm was set to yield the wage indicated by skill and industry classification.

The procedure for rate-setting is familiar in any industrial concern, capitalist or socialist, although, with the trade union compliant to management and to the local official of the communist party, the process of revising norms usually left the worker a lesser share of the increment in labour productivity than he would have gained under union-led bargaining. The nation-wide comparison of the skill-content of jobs was unique to the centrally-planned economies and was competently executed, but, like the industrial ranking, the central authorities found themselves unable subsequently to make structural revisions: to change norms within individual factories was one matter, to vary the priority of whole industries was another.

The flexible adjustment of a market economy being renounced, alterations in skill or industry differentials had to be made by explicit government decision, and proposals aroused the opposition of the ministries whose industry would have been disfavoured. The plan priorities of the early 'fifties—with, notably, mining and metallurgy at the head and consumers' goods and services at the foot—have thus tended to persist. The three countries with market principles in view have, as might be expected, led in wage reform. A serious attempt was made in Hungary in 1964 and in Czechoslovakia in 1968 to re-structure the industrial differentials for basic wages, in favour respectively of export-orientated and of consumer-goods sectors, and a more modest reform was begun in Bulgaria in 1969. Elsewhere, adaptation to new planning priorities is made only within an aggregate wage increase scheduled in an annual plan from expected rises in industrial productivity.

The basic wage accounts in the industry of the six countries for between three-quarters and four-fifths of total operatives' earnings, the balance being due to over-fulfilment of piecenorms, or to other bonuses. Job or collective premia fall, in the directive system, within the centrally-determined financial dispositions, which leave little—though rarely no—scope for inter-enterprise competition for skills which are scarce at the going wage.

Wages have not in any eastern European country assured supply-demand equilibrium by skill or branch, and in order to attract and keep skilled or semi-skilled labour, managers have often had to overgrade individual positions if they wished to avoid under-staffing or high labour turnover. 'Wage drift', so generated, has also been caused by the reduction of working hours and the consequent increase in overtime payments; while this is not unusual in a west European context, it is contrary to the Soviet practice of permitting overtime only in exceptional circumstances.

The labour market is free in the sense that no compulsion is exercised on choice of employment, but collective bargaining is limited by the preclusion of the strike. Workers seek to take advantage of scarcities by frequent moves from job to job, a tendency only weakly offset by the grant of long-service bonuses by the enterprises, and by the control over movements from town to town exercised by the system of municipal residence permits. In 1968, both Czechoslovakia and Rumania introduced 'loyalty premia', personal bonuses related to the period worked in the same enterprise.

Price determination

Price control during the war and post-war reconstruction was everywhere the progenitor of a state committee for prices, one of the arms of the central authorities. Its staff was never large, ranging from about one hundred in Czechoslovakia to half-a-dozen in Albania—a small establishment was typical also of the Soviet Union (90); nor was its chairman anything other than a civil-service administrator—certainly not an economic policy-maker. There is some parallel with wartime Britain, where the Central Price Regulation Committee was a small body, the names of whose members were unfamiliar to the public. Not until economic reform did the office gain in stature (the appointments in Hungary and Rumania were particularly notable). Modest staff and leadership were consistent with the ranking of price policy as a supplement to plan implementation by direct order.

Operational prices had been only one, and not the most weighty, of a number of information carriers employed by the central authorities, which did not hold it essential for prices to effect an equilibrium between supply and demand, i.e. at the level of prices they determined effective demand need not be met, or supply might be left excessive for the demand. Since the former usually prevailed, rationing of raw materials was enforced and enterprises had difficulty with deliveries of equipment and machinery. Most countries, not only those where the directive system is being dismantled, are trying to establish a level of prices at which raw materials and other producers' goods will be in supply-demand equilibrium. When the first medium-term plans were drawn up the application of mathematical methods and electronic data-processing was unknown as techniques for determining programming prices for a vast network of planned transactions or for testing the effect of proposed changes in operational prices. Just as the need to pass orders up and down a hierarchy for lateral contracts to be established between enterprises caused inter-factory transactions to be perpetuated long after the rationale for the exchanges had passed, so the restricted potential of the state price committee caused prices to be constant for far too long.

The inflexibility of operational prices was incidental to Soviet practice, whereas the formula according to which they were determined—wholly dependent upon input costs—was a fundamental shortcoming. It was based upon an interpretation of Marx's 'labour theory of value' which excluded his 'use-value', viz. that conditioned by demand factors; it was strictly supply-orientated, formed of 'self-cost' (wages, current materials and a charge for the depreciation of assets) plus profit as a variable proportion thereto at the discretion of price controllers.

The three other formulae discussed in preparation for east European economic reform are intended to bring order into the profit supplement—seen as an expression of Marxian 'surplus value' for the redistribution of national product from

86

the primary creators of value. A 'value price' restricts profit to a proportion of wages alone, but has not been used in any country, although it was seriously considered in Bulgaria for the price reform begun in 1969; the 'production price' relates profit to capital assets employed in production, and is that used in the Hungarian reform of 1968; and the 'two-channel model', employed for the Czechoslovak reform of 1967, calculates profit as the sum of differentiated proportions of capital and of wages. The Bulgarian price reform will, it is understood, retain the ratio to 'self-cost', subject, like those in the two countries adopting the guided market economy, to some adaptation to prices ruling abroad. In Hungary a 'foreign-trade multiplier' (see page 79) was used to link those prices with domestic ones, while there and in Bulgaria customs duties are now charged to all state enterprises, hitherto exempt.

Bulgaria, Czechoslovakia and Hungary are seeking—both through the reflection of foreign-trade price ratios and a market relationship between domestic enterprises—to assure the penetration of demand conditions to price formation. Neither of the latter envisage any more 'price reforms'—co-ordinated revisions of all wholesale prices—which will be unnecessary when a market mechanism prevails. In 1969 Bulgaria began a price reform (scheduled in 1966 for 1968) both to align prices more closely to world ratios and to introduce some elements of a market through the 'inter-enterprise agreement' system (as described in the preceding chapter), but the pricing commission will, declaredly, be prepared to veto price changes by enterprises which seem detrimental to the consumer—through monopoly—or to the interests of the state.

In all three countries, Bulgaria, Czechoslovakia and Hungary, the distinction is drawn between prices which are fixed, those which may fluctuate subject to a maximum and those which are wholly free. In Czechoslovakia price liberalisation was begun in 1967 when prices relating to 4 per cent of transactions in domestically-produced capital goods and raw materials were wholly freed and 80 per cent allowed to fluctuate within limits. By the end of the first year 13 per cent of consumer-goods transactions were free, with the remainder staying fixed, but it was planned during 1968 to raise the unrestricted proportion to 20 per cent and allow a further 20 per cent to vary within upper and lower limits. The cautious policy on reform necessitated by the invasion and the serious inflationary pressure of 1969 resulted in the reimposition of virtually total price-control, not officially by the Board for Prices but informally by the Czech and Slovak Boards for Industry.

Hungary, on the other hand, has greatly extended market pricing since January 1968. Eighteen months later, 80 per cent of the prices of capital goods were free (with the remainder either fixed or subject to maxima), as were 40 per cent of domestically-produced raw materials. Among controlled raw materials, fixed prices were still being set for fuel and power and for basic commodities, while other goods (including those for which conditions of imperfect competition may prevail) were subject to maxima. The pace of decontrol for consumers' goods is shown in the following table, but it is to be noted that the 50 per cent of items which will be fixed or under ceilings in 1971 constitute three-quarters of the basket for the cost-of-living index. Some rise in the latter is to be expected, but the profit-sharing schemes introduced by the reforms (see page 124) are intended to lead to real-wage increment. In a particular case—pharmaceuticals obtained on prescription—the price now paid at retail is 15 per cent of list price, the balance being met by the buyer's trade-union social insurance; when prices become entirely free it is planned to raise the percentage payment by the user to 30 per cent but to counter the higher actual cost by reducing turnover tax.

Within the countries retaining the directive system, and hence controlled pricing, the differences lie in which of four groups of agency prices are fixed—a central specialist body, ministries, industrial associations and local authorities. The

DETERMINATION OF CONSUMER-GOODS PRICES
IN HUNGARY
(percentage of transactions)

	1968	1969	Expected 1971
Fixed	20	15	10
Maxima	30	35	40
Sub-total	50	50	50
With upper and lower limits	27	20	0
Free	23	30	50
Sub-total	50	50	50

greatest devolution from a central body has been shown, since 1967, in the GDR. Nearly two-thirds of all wholesale prices are set by the VVBs under only general supervision by the Government Commission for Prices, and about one-third by ministries; the exiguous remainder are determined by *bezirk* and *kreis* authorities, who also have jurisdiction over prices charged by private industry. The vast majority of prices are classified as *fest* (firm), but upon which some negotiation—within 5 per cent either way—can be entertained by either buyer or seller; they are not constant for excessively long, those of the 1964–7 revision being reviewed in 1969–70. A small but growing set of prices are defined as *vereinbarung* (agreement), in use for complete plant, custom-made equipment and special products, where both sides are free to bargain, or as maxima, where demand and supply at that price are unbalanced but where the Commission for Prices is unwilling to sanction a higher price or to benefit sellers. The Commission proposes to maintain 'firm' prices wherever VVB positions appear monopolistic. Describing the second stage of the economic reform to a meeting of the Party Central Committee on 7 June 1968, a member of the Politburo emphasised that 'price development remains firmly in the hands of the state and that no spontaneous and free price formation is permitted'. The modifications thus go no way towards market pricing for wholesaling; prices in retail shops and those paid to collectives and farmers for agricultural procurements remain centrally-determined.

The Polish procedure, as effective in 1968, is highly centralised, with ratification by the Council of Ministers required for the wholesale prices of key industrial goods and the state procurement prices of milk, grain, meat and potatoes from private farms. Ministries set wholesale prices for the majority of producers' goods, and for one consumers' goods, books, which is heavily subsidised. The Commission for Prices determines the retail prices of all products manufactured by industries under central direction, and the prices of certain goods made by industries subordinate to regional authorities (*voivodships*). At the level of regional planning authorities, regional price commissions determine retail prices for goods manufactured by industries under voivodship control and set maximum prices for fruit and vegetables sold by private farmers. The Central Co-operative Organisation is authorised to fix its own prices, and retailing enterprises are allowed to determine the prices of the goods they buy from private farmers and artisans, as well as the selling price of fruit and vegetables. The particular seller and buyer determine in negotiations the prices of goods for export, of products individually ordered, or of subcontracted items and components. A new price reform is being prepared, for introduction with the next five-year plan (1971–5), but, as already indicated (page 66), may undermine the projected profitability of draft plans concurrently being formulated by industrial associations in terms of current aggregative prices.

The balance of power between the industrial ministries and the special price committees has shifted in opposite directions in Albania and Rumania. In 1966 the rights of Albanian ministries and local authorities to set prices for their enterprises were greatly enlarged—to cover 80 per cent of all prices —and the prices themselves generally revised. On the other hand, since the decision by the Rumanian government at the end of 1967 to introduce economic reform, the authority of the price committee has grown (signified by the successive appointment to its chairmanship of former Vice-Presidents of the Planning Committee), but there is still some indecision on price policy. A four-to-five year period between wholesale price revisions had been envisaged when the 1963 reform was complete, but, though being prepared, no changes had been made six years later. The Party resolutions of 1967 on the principles of reform envisaged that some wholesale price-fixing should be devolved to industrial associations, but no such powers were incorporated into their statute when enacted in April 1969.

Taxation

All countries save Albania and Rumania now levy a charge on capital assets, which is described in the context of enterprise financial dispositions (pages 109–25). The absence of a charge on capital (supplied to state enterprises by non-reimbursable grant from the public exchequer) had been a major weakness of Soviet-type price formation, while the employment of shadow pricing had affected only decisions on new investment. Hungary introduced in 1968 a rent payable to the state for the use by enterprises of industrial sites: it amounts to 5 per cent of the value of the site, but transitional maxima were allowed to ease the burden in 1968 and 1969 —the sum actually paid could not exceed 0·2 and 0·4 per cent respectively of the value of fixed assets.

The margin between operational wholesale and retail prices (other than that due to distributors' mark-ups, transport and similar costs) is absorbed in the directive system by turnover tax, for which there were hence as many rates as there were prices. Thus there were in Hungary more than 2500 turnover tax rates and several tens of thousands of 'differential tax items' levied as a difference between wholesale and retail price; in Czechoslovakia there were as many as $1\frac{1}{2}$ million such differentials.

Both countries, as a consequence of adopting their 1967 and 1968 reforms, are consolidating these rates into a set similar to the indirect taxes of a standard market economy: there will be eventually 1200 in Czechoslovakia and as few as 300–400 in Hungary (against 1000 after the major revisions of 1968). By tying the movements of retail prices to those of wholesale prices, where before they moved separately, a crucial step was taken to reflect consumer preference in the prices facing the industrial supplier.

7
Directives or Competition

THE INDUSTRIAL association is the institution which distinguishes the east European directive systems from the Soviet type. The reforms promulgated in the USSR in 1965 make no provision for this entity between enterprise and the central authorities, although many 'unions' (*obedinenie*) and 'firms' (*firmy*) have been created *ad hoc*. Except in Albania and Hungary the industrial association sets a wide range of compulsory targets for its enterprises: differences occur in the relationship of the association to the ministry with respect to the interests of those enterprises.

Negotiation of enterprise targets

In Poland, during the negotiation of targets with the industrial ministry, officials of the association tend to take the part of their constituent enterprises, but when targets for the association have been ratified by the ministry, the situation is reversed and the association and its enterprises view each other as opponents. The association is concerned to obtain the 'easiest' plan for its enterprises, but its managers are remunerated by premia related to enterprises' plan fulfilment once the plan is in operation. Even when the plan is current, however, enterprises may prevail upon the association to seek a revision of targets: thus in 1967 the Association for the Iron and Steel Industry successfully applied on three occasions to the Ministry of Heavy Industry to reduce the planned profit target, lowering it from an original 6·18 per cent to 5·02 per cent by successive stages of 5·97 and 5·20. Some changes have to be made in the plans approved because the schedule for drawing up the targets allows little time for thorough verification of their mutual consistency, let alone a review of the variant options open to each enterprise.

It requires the State Planning Commission's guide-lines for

industrial ministries and voivodship councils to be completed by the end of May: until the end of August the ministries negotiate with associations, whence a draft national plan is aggregated and checked for broad consistency so that it may be approved by the Council of Ministers during the second half of October; industrial associations have three weeks from the date of approval to elaborate targets for their subordinate enterprises, which have a further month (to mid-December) to draw up their individual plans (the 'technical, production and financial plan', *plan TPF*), which should be internally consistent. The plan is finally confirmed by the Council of Ministers, and approved by the Sejm (Parliament); any changes resulting from debates in those bodies are then communicated to associations and thence to enterprises. In practice, as already mentioned, the time limits are not always respected, and the plan to which an enterprise works in the first quarter of the year is in some instances provisional, and may deviate quite considerably from the quarterly division of the annual plan as finally confirmed.

The German VVB receives its indicators from the industrial ministries (during 1964–5 from the industrial department of the State Economic Council, dissolved at the end of 1965), but appears to be rather readier than the Polish associations to take the part of its enterprises, because the volume of profit earned by the VVB as a whole is more important than the fulfilment of the detailed indicators handed down by the central authorities. Partnership between VVB and enterprise is stressed by their joint responsibility for the sale of products and for efficient marketing abroad: the VVB collaborates with the Ministries of Domestic and of Foreign Trade in the analysis of demand other than from state production enterprises, the 'material balances' serving as guides for inter-industry requirements. The sense of partnership is, however, limited to current transactions, because the VVB has considerable (and until 1967 full) control over funds for investment—new capital, self-finance from profits and depreciation charges.

In Bulgaria control by ministries over industrial associations varies considerably by branch. Thus, until the codification of 1969 which put the limit at seven targets, the 'Farmachim' pharmaceutical amalgamation was given ten sets of directives by its ministry which it broke down to enterprises—physical output of specified products, export and import quotas in values, investment ceilings, quotas for raw materials supplied from domestic sources and a group of financial constraints set out as a ratio to the value of gross revenue, viz. the wage-bill, outlays on technical development and on new products, and on the bonus and social fund. The Rodopa food-processing amalgamation, on the other hand, was given as target merely a sum of profit and of foreign-exchange to be earned; its business is highly export-orientated and is hence less controlled than the pharmaceutical industry, which operates largely for the domestic market, and, protected against foreign competition, doubtless has fewer in-built incentives to efficiency.

The Rumanian industrial association establishes compulsory targets for its enterprises, but those which it receives from the ministry are described in the Statute (promulgated in April 1969) as 'orientational' and it is required to take account of enterprise proposals in formulating targets which eventually form part of the ministry's indicators, the fulfilment of which is the association's responsibility. Its powers over investment are complete; it is directly responsible for the building of new enterprises in its branch and for all capital work in existing plants, and it has full rights over the supplies to, and sales of, its enterprises. While the authority of the association seems preponderant vis-à-vis its enterprises, the presence on its board of directors of the managers of all its constituents must guarantee some participation: the principle of 'collective management' is stressed in the Statute and the fact that only one of the board is a representative of the trade union for the branch implies that decisions taken will tend to be 'management oriented'.

It was such powers of redistributing funds for investment

among enterprises within the Czechoslovak association which led to the demand for the enterprise to be allowed to resign its membership; promised in the halcyon days before August, the right was on the point of being granted in early 1969, but is unlikely to figure in any eventual definitive 'Law on the Enterprise'. The associations (mostly constituted by combination in a product-group) were strongly criticised during 1968 for monopolistic practices, and for perpetuating the practices of administrative planning, in defiance of market requirements, by arranging with industrial ministries special advantages for their product. Their power to redistribute profits among their enterprises was formally withdrawn at the end of that year, but, as indicated elsewhere (page 69) they have resumed the issue of instructions to enterprises as an 'emergency measure'.

Compulsory associations have no long-run part in the Hungarian reform, but ministries have the right to oblige enterprises to form a union for a period not exceeding five years. This power was exercised to replace some associations dissolved in 1968, but it is not a serious constraint on enterprise autonomy, for no union can impose instructions on constituents, and its authority is limited to the terms of its contract of association. At the same time a number of regulations were issued against monopolistic agreements between enterprises, notably prohibiting market-sharing, price maintenance and limitation on entry, and requiring 'early warning' of price increases. The associations now tend to be vertical (grouping successive stages in the process of production) rather than horizontal (uniting the same stage of production), many of the latter existing before the reform not being re-established.

When the Albanian planning system was simplified in 1966 —without changes deep enough to be termed an economic reform—the major amendment for industry lay in the abrogation by the State Planning Commission (with ratification by the Council of Ministers) of annual distribution quotas ('plan for material-technical supply'). Since 1966 it only sets out allotments by ministry (viz. to industry, agriculture, construction, trade and communications), which affect the distribution to their enterprises under quarterly plans. The number of indicators entering the enterprise plan was at the same time decreased.

Foreign trade

The market orientation of the Czechoslovak and the Hungarian reforms would allow associations (or even substantial enterprises) to gain a monopoly with relative ease, because the scale of plant is for technical and historical reasons large, while the home market is small. Each government, therefore, determined to admit foreign goods to the extent that the threat of imports was necessary to maintain competitiveness. In Czechoslovakia the foreign-trade monopoly was not broken, as the reformers had confidently expected, although the rigid pattern of foreign-trade corporations was attenuated when, during 1968 and 1969, joint companies with the participation both of producers and foreign-trade agencies began to be created; from 1969 any enterprise or co-operative may be granted, subject to certain conditions, a permit to trade abroad. In Hungary domestic enterprises have not been given the general right to engage in trade abroad, but they may be individually authorised to transact in a specific line. Until 1957 the pattern was the same as elsewhere in eastern Europe, i.e. foreign-trade corporations monopolised all exchanges with foreign partners. In that year seven producers were permitted to export on their own account, but numbers were not significantly enlarged until the reform in January 1968; by 1969 over a hundred enterprises (including the forty or so foreign-trade corporations) were in operation on foreign markets.

In Hungary there remains the former arrangement whereby a foreign-trade corporation buys from the producers or sells to them at its own risk; the difference from past practice is that the trade enterprise can no longer buy at a fixed price, but must negotiate the purchase price of an export or the selling price of an import and work for profit: like all enterprises, those engaged in foreign trade must operate within certain regulations and bear taxes on profits; many of the former foreign-trade corporations nevertheless operate not on their own account but on commission from production enterprises. There are two new forms of contractual relationships between interested parties: under one the trading and producing partners have a common interest in the profits on the transaction abroad, and under the second a minimum export price is agreed by each and profit-sharing does not take place until after a certain agreed mark-up on that minimum price has been assured.

Bulgaria has gone little beyond an expression of hope in competition, but the 1969 customs duties allow the government to vary the degree of protection accorded when monopoly power is considered a danger. Though bound by commitments in non-tariff terms to Comecon, it is not tied by undertakings to GATT, and if the pending applications to GATT by Hungary and Rumania are agreed (Czechoslovakia and Poland already being members but the GDR still politically unacceptable), Bulgaria will be the sole nonparticipant nation of the group. The considerable extent of foreign-trading authority allowed to certain amalgamations since April 1966 has just been noted (page 95).

A few months after the introduction of the Bulgarian regulations a new and similar plan indicator was defined in the GDR for VVBs and enterprises engaged in export, viz. the difference between foreign earnings (converted by a specified co-efficient) and the domestic cost. Each VVB is given a quota for importing, which varies with the fulfilment of the net earnings indicator. The GDR is thus midway between Bulgaria and Rumania, where some industrial enterprises keep that part of export earnings exceeding the plan target, and Hungary where the government has set itself against any such retention.

Foreign trade cannot be the sole answer to the monopoly ower inherent in product-defined associations. A resolution f the Bulgarian Communist Party of July 1968—ushering in second phase of economic reform—stated that conditions 1ould be established for the 'correct use of the market 1echanism' and for 'more active economic competition' be-ween individual enterprises, 'to eliminate the deleterious ffects of the monopoly position of certain enterprises and malgamations'. The threat to import is somewhat empty, evertheless, as long as all the main trading countries have eavy balance-of-payments deficits with convertible-currency artners.

Import authorisation, in principle, resides in the central ank or Ministry of Finance which allocates foreign exchange, ave in the earnings retention schemes of some Bulgarian, :zechoslovak, German and Rumanian enterprises. Hungary as already merged the allocation of foreign exchange with 1e issue of import licences (the National Bank assuring ex-hange for any licence approved), but in January 1968 it nposed an import-deposit scheme appreciably stiffer than 1e British requirement of the same year: a deposit of oo per cent (for the year 1968, 150 per cent) of the value of ny machine to be imported, must be made and is held for wo years without payment of interest. The procedure is cer-ainly better than the foreign-exchange quota system operat-1g elsewhere in eastern Europe where the strength of the 1ppressed demands for imports—especially for techno-1gically-advanced machinery—cannot be gauged.

Other measures proposed to counter the monopoly power f industrial associations include the retention of central price xing, the deliberate exclusion of some enterprises from the 1dustrial association and the imposition on associations of :gulations which would of themselves inhibit such actions he 'rules of the game' approach which Lange advocated for oland but which have not been developed into any practical 1rm). It may well be that the competitive structure of

99

industry in some countries is such that a sellers' market canno
but operate at any price acceptable on social grounds, an
that the policy of 'concentration and specialisation' under
taken over the past fifteen years has resulted in a domesti
monopoly for single plants. The dissolution of the industria
associations in such circumstances would still leave *de fact*
monopolies. Clearly the specialisation and concentration cam
paign would not have gone as far as it had without yielding
some economies of scale, which would be forfeited if
deliberate policy of de-concentration or duplication of pro
duction were undertaken.

The compulsory 'indicators'

In the guided market economy, the eventual role of the
industrial association is to service its member enterprise
(research and development, design, market analysis, adver
tising etc.) and to engage in medium- and long-run indicative
planning which would bridge the gap between, and be avail
able to, member-enterprises and the central authorities. In
the more prevalent directive system such functions are out
weighed by its role in setting targets. The extreme form i
its specification in physical units of what its enterprises mus
produce, in a plan for what is termed 'nomenclature' o
'assortment'. An inquiry conducted by the former Economi
Council in Poland during 1956–9 showed that all output i
enterprises under the Ministry of Light Industry was deter
mined by the assortment plan, and almost all (94 per cent
was so dictated in enterprises under the Ministry of Foo
Industry; three-quarters of output under the Ministry o
Heavy Industry was thus determined, but the corresponding
share in the Ministry of Chemical Industry was little mor
than half. Of the 315 enterprises which completed th
questionnaire only eight declared that the share of impose
product-mix was less than a quarter of output, a mere thir
teen had less than 50 per cent imposed and seventeen les
than 80 per cent, leaving the overwhelming majority (277
subject to dictation of their detailed output-patterns for four

ifths of their production. The lower the degree of product-mix control the more able is an enterprise to adapt to the demand of others (for producers' goods) or of the retail market (for consumers' goods).

In addition to its 'success indicators' the enterprise under directive practice has to accord a certain degree of weight to informational indicators', because the association draws them up in the light of the directives it receives and will correspondingly exercise pressure on its constituents. Both types of indicator have hence to be incorporated in the enterprise's technical, production and financial plan' (*orgtekhplan* in Bulgaria, *PFI-plan* in the GDR, *plan TPF* in Poland and *plan t.i.f.* in Rumania). Inconsistencies must be resolved by negotiation with the association, and in contractual negotiation with supplying and recipient enterprises, but, once ratified by the association, the plan is binding with respect to output and product-mix, except where it can be over-fulfilled within the limits of materials-allocation and employment, and provided that the higher output can be sold; the enterprise may also fail to fulfil the planned product-mix if it can prove to the satisfaction of the association that no demand existed for the planned output.

The imposition of more than one indicator upon an enterprise requires the supervising authority to make its assessment from outside, based upon whatever inspection, report, negotiation or consultation it may demand. Any inconsistency between two or more such directives should, moreover, be resolved on the initiative of the enterprise when it draws up its technical, production and financial plan, but, as already indicated (page 75), enterprises prefer to leave themselves a certain slack. Polish experience shows that there is relatively little looseness in setting the assortment plan while it ranks high among the indicators upon which managerial bonuses are calculated. An examination of the twenty-four consecutive quarterly plans from the beginning of 1957 to the end of 1961 in the Otmęt (Silesia) shoe factory, showed that deviation from the assortment plan exceeded 5 per cent on only two occasions; in the majority of cases it was less than 1 per cent. The deviation from the profit plan, on the other hand, in three separate quarters exceeded 100 per cent and in two instances 200 per cent; divergence by more than 30 (but less than 100) per cent took place on nine occasions. Plans for supplies (an 'informational indicator') ranked in magnitude between these two extremes: there were nine quarters when the deviation of deliveries from plan was 10 or more per cent in the case of leather for soles, and on eight occasions in the case of leather for uppers; deliveries were within $1\frac{1}{2}$ per cent of expectation on only two occasions for sole leather and on one occasion for upper leather.

The lack of realism (in the sense of conformity to projection) in profit planning was indicated more recently in the findings of a special sub-committee set up in 1968 by the Polish Party Central Committee: of 533 enterprises (spread among twenty-five industrial associations) less than one in five showed a profit fulfilment of 5 per cent above or below the target; the majority (284 enterprises) were between 5 and 50 per cent above or below their planned profits, but there were still some which showed what the sub-committee called 'pathological deviation' in excess of 50 per cent, with a variation from only 10 per cent to six times the target profit. Among the reasons for these deviations cited by the sub-committee were the unreliability of raw-material supply, changes in deadline for the completion of investment and in difference among both industrial associations and enterprise in fixing a profit target: it was generally believed, based on past experience, that the profit plan would be adjusted during the year to conform to actual performance if the other obligatory plan indicators (above all, the assortment plan) were fulfilled.

To counter this indifference and the deliberate insertion of slack, and to derive other indicators from the one initially chosen, the central authorities compute relationships within a branch (or even an individual enterprise) by three methods: 'technologically-determined norms', based upon detailed studies or expert projections of specific industrial processes, statistically-determined norms', extrapolations of past performance, but incorporating their assumptions on the future, and 'estimated norms' or informed guesses. Most relationships are of the two latter kind, but to force management to improve its performance they are frequently adapted as 'progressive norms', which require, say, a tighter ratio of input than in the previous year (an example of what has been termed the 'ratchet principle').

The indicator to which norms were applied to derive, or check upon, others used either to be a target in physical terms or the 'global value of output'. The latter is defined as all production within the enterprise during a stated period: frequently translated as 'gross production' (from the Bulgarian *obshchyata produktsiya*, the Czech *hrubá výroba*, the German *Bruttoproduktion* and the Russian *valovaya produktsiya*), a better form is 'global', the literal form used in Albanian, Polish and Rumanian, and corresponding to the Hungarian *teljes termelési érték*, because the conventional economic meaning of 'gross' is 'without deduction of depreciation' (as distinct from 'net', after deduction of depreciation). If the turnover is of finished goods only (viz. excluding any increment in stocks of semi-fabricates), the term is 'commodity production' (from the Russian *tovarnaya produktsiya*) but output so defined is now employed as an 'indicator' only in Poland (*produkcja towarowa*) and Rumania (*producţia marfă*), qualified in the latter that the goods must be 'sold and paid for' along the lines of the new indicator for Soviet enterprises of 'production sold' (*realizovannaya produktsiya*).

The most glaring of the deficiencies of 'global' product as a measure of enterprise activity was its inclusion of materials bought from other enterprises. Plan fulfilment could, for example, be achieved with fewer products than planned if suitably offset by an above-plan input of materials (each machine would contain more metal or a coat more cloth) or by manufacturing more complete products than planned but fewer spare parts (a tractor, say, added more to global output because its selling price comprised more outside materials than parts made in the plant concerned).

An indicator of global production, early castigated as 'tonnenideologie' by the Party First Secretary in the GDR, is still employed in Poland and Rumania. It was the principal —often the sole—determinant of the plan in Albania until 1967, when the assortment index was promoted to parity with it; in early 1969 the Chairman of the Albanian Planning Commission stated reasons for dissatisfaction with the global index, but has not yet dispensed with its use. A Polish inquiry of 1964 showed that it was used in 82 per cent of enterprises (which produced 77 per cent of total industrial output). Its retention, despite formal abolition as the determinant indicator of the enterprise plan, testifies to the qualities which commended it to the central planning authorities—ease of calculation, additivity at all levels of administration and universal applicability in industry; though no longer the determinant of the plan, global output remains in Albania and Poland a condition for the payment of managerial premia and the basis for computing the wage-fund ceiling.

Goals in physical units supplement or replace global-value targets and usually appear as product-mix assignments. The degree of their proliferation is difficult to assess; all commodities which figure in central material balances appear as physical-output or assortment indicators for some enterprises. Balances used in this way continue in Albania (for about 100 products), Bulgaria (for 132), the GDR (for 168), Rumania (for 232) and Poland (for 430). The number of items cited for a recent year, relate only to those on central 'material balances'; thus there were a further 1200 items in other Rumanian balances, and in the GDR, 2128 in the *sortimentabilanz* under a VVB(Z) and 47 under a VVB(B) while controls tantamount to an output plan were exercised by distribution services, which established 'supplementary balances' (*Ergänzungsbilanzen*) for 1737 items through the state wholesale agencies (*Staatliche kontore*) and for 28 items through other bodies. Such less important items may be entered in product-mix targets, but others are listed solely for purposes of allocation. On the other hand, items which are not included in a planned balance may be isolated as 'priority' targets for certain enterprises, and for certain uses. Bulgaria uses an indicator of 'volume of production of items under the inter-enterprise agreement system' (see page 69).

An alternative measure of enterprise activity is the summation of man-hour inputs (the *zeitsummenmethode* of the GDR), and the Polish use of the Soviet equivalent, the 'normative value of processing'. Whereas in Poland in 1963 only 1·6 per cent of enterprises (producing 7 per cent of global industrial output) had success indicators in physical units, enterprises making 11 per cent of output were assessed on the 'normative' procedure. This excludes from the value adopted for enterprise indicators both profits and the bulk of inputs, leaving only 'normed' labour costs, fuel costs, depreciation and overheads. Its experimental use in the USSR (mainly in the garment-making industry) was intended by its proponents to counter the rival advocacy of Liberman (Professor at Kharkov University) of 'profitability', defined as the profits of an enterprise as a ratio of its stock of fixed and working capital. In the Soviet reform, begun in 1966 and applied by the end of 1968 to 27,000 industrial enterprises (accounting for 72 per cent of global output and over four-fifths of aggregate profits), Liberman's 'profitability'—which he had urged as a sole 'synthetic' indicator—was introduced as only one of eight targets imposed upon the enterprise (the others being 'production sold', a product-mix, the wage-bill, tax payments, material inputs or input–output ratios and assignments for new technology and for capital investment). A minimum profit has been adopted as a compulsory indicator in the GDR and Rumania and was used between 1966 and 1968 in Bulgaria; three related ratios are in use in Poland, viz. 'net profitability' (profit as a ratio of total cost of goods sold), 'gross profitability' (profit plus turnover tax in the same ratio) and 'rate of profit' (profit as a ratio of the value of fixed and working capital).

Present practice includes, also, among compulsory indicators others currently used in the USSR—tax payments (or subsidies) in Albania and Poland; maxima for the consumption of specified materials (or input–output ratios) in Bulgaria, the GDR and Poland; a maximum wage-bill as a ratio to gross income in Bulgaria and as an absolute limit, with an employment ceiling in Poland (where breakdowns by operative, administrative and technical staff and their corresponding employment quotas are also laid down); investment limits and directives for technological change in Bulgaria and Poland (at the association and the enterprise level respectively). Of indicators no longer obligatory to the USSR, cost of production (for items comparable to any produced in the previous year) is still used in Albania, the GDR, Poland and Rumania, while labour productivity (global output per operative) continues explicitly in Albania, Poland and Rumania. Indicators relating to foreign-trade performance are not used in the largely self-sufficient USSR, but are in use in Bulgaria, the GDR and Poland.

8
Finance

EASTERN EUROPEAN governments—that of Albania always
excepted—are now looking at their economies as Alfred P.
Sloan saw General Motors in 1923, for his principles of
division into profit centres coupled with strict financial supervision are basic to all their varieties of reform. To the in-
herited methods of proprietorial capitalism can be matched
those of directive planning: the problem of the 'legacy' of the
Soviet-type mechanism (first argued by Neuberger) has indeed rapidly come to the fore in the analysis of contemporary
change.

Locating the profit centre

The Hungarian reform and the intended developments in
Czechoslovakia stand out as the examples of devolution to
the enterprise as profit centre, with taxation and a statutory
mechanism controlling finance. In the four other countries,
the industrial association increasingly finances its group opera-
tions from earnings. In the absence of a capital market—one
of the crucial distinctions from the Yugoslav system since
1965, but the embryo of which can be perceived in Hungary
—funds for expanding industries are taken from the others
through taxation and channelled back (save in Rumania)
through bank credit.

The legacy of centralism can explain the persistence of
directives in countries where associations have been constituted as a bureaucratic compromise, but it is equally con-
vincing to interpret direct government instruction as an offset
to potential monopoly power and to continuing imperfections
in prices as information-carriers. At present the dividing line
between the directive system and the guided market puts
the predominance of the association in the one and of the
enterprise in the other; in Bulgaria, which tends to the latter,

but with continuing directives, the enterprise is stronger vis-à-vis its association than in the four countries of the first-named group. There is no reason—allowing for safeguards against monopoly—why associations should not come to enjoy the same financial autonomy as enterprises in Hungary today. Some management experts in eastern Europe, after study of western experience, believe that their industrial sectors have too small a base to permit the individual enterprise to be a profit centre: for them efficiency lies in concentration upon the model of the capitalist corporation. The authority over capital finance of the VVB in the GDR at present and that with which associations in Poland and Rumania have been endowed with effect from 1966 and 1970 respectively suggest that this view is gaining ground.

However that trend may be, the distinction among the reforms so far implemented lies in the authority of the enterprise to dispose of its profit or gross revenue (value-added, viz. receipts from sales less depreciation and payments to other enterprises for goods and services), upon which, together with loans repayable from expected profits, it depends for all its current and capital needs. In those countries maintaining a directive system, the distribution of profit is determined on an annual basis and in conformity with a plan by administrative decision for each enterprise separately; self-finance is hence virtually unrelated to the pattern of prices facing the enterprise and to the latter's performance; a planned investment is executed—with funds from the Exchequer, the banks or other enterprises (through the association) —whether or not income from enterprise activity is sufficient. In the same way, the arbitrary variation in the authorisation of self-finance precludes independent planning by the enterprise over any extended period. Before the various reforms there had been little finance of investment from an enterprise's own resources, but since the changes the allowance has not only increased but may be substantially supplemented by loans from the banking system, repayable with interest out of the income derived from the investment.

The introduction of the guided market economy, first, eliminates any such targets; secondly, it increases the share of self-finance and bank loans in capital formation by existing enterprises; thirdly, it almost completely suppresses investment subsidies (whether from the Ministry of Finance or an industrial association); and lastly, it replaces financial norms fixed for the individual enterprise and varied year by year by taxes the rates of which are enacted beforehand and should run for periods longer than a year. The enterprise depends for its operation upon its earnings—gross revenue in Bulgaria and Czechoslovakia, profit in Hungary—which determine, above guaranteed wage minima, the remuneration of all staff. In Bulgaria the imposition of targets continues (though their number was reduced in 1968)—with premia paid as these are fulfilled—but in the other two states government powers for a directive system are seen as reapplicable only for exceptional use. Hungary is patently furthest advanced towards a market economy, but the determinate distribution of profit by superior authority distinguishes its system from the freedom of the Yugoslav firm.

No two countries within either group have the same financial dispositions, which are hence more clearly describable by country, grouped into those where directives predominate and those where the aim is decentralised financial autonomy. In all states, payment of turnover tax (almost entirely confined to consumers' goods) is a separate transaction and need only formally be considered part of the taxes on revenue.

Directive finance

POLAND

The Polish industrial enterprise has three charges to pay from those of its outlays classified as 'cost': to transfer to its association a specified share of depreciation charges, and to allocate a given percentage mark-up on its production cost for the general costs of the association (the 'association fund'), and to finance a 'technical development fund' run by the industrial association. It has three obligations on its profit: to pay interest on its fixed capital to the Ministry of Finance, to establish the 'factory fund' from which shares in profit are distributed to all staff, and to make over a given share in its profit to the association. Under these arrangements about four-fifths of enterprise profit and two-thirds of depreciation charges are transferred to higher authorities. In practice little more than the amount of the annual depreciation charge which is required for 'capital repairs' (major maintenance and repair work, as opposed to 'current repairs', which are financed as part of cost) is left at the disposal of the enterprise; the bulk of depreciation charges, earmarked for the replacement of capital assets, is subject to allocation by the industrial association or Ministry of Finance.

In the plan for 1966–70 a mere 9 per cent of total investment is being financed by enterprises. Excluding from total investment that in construction projects not yet functioning as a production enterprise, industrial investment in 1962 was only 40 per cent self-financed (from depreciation charges and profits), 10 per cent was borrowed from the banking system, while half came from grants from the Ministry of Finance or the industrial association. Some relaxation has since taken place in the authority of the enterprise to increase the supply of consumer services by removing limitations on employment in that branch, but the maximum for the wage-bill remains. In engineering and chemicals, enterprises have to make payments to a 'fund for new production' in addition to the 'technical development fund'. The tax on capital is confined to fixed assets, working capital being exempt. The rate varies from zero to $2\frac{1}{2}$ and 5 per cent of the value of assets and the allocation to the 'factory fund' is a share of the wage-bill specified for each enterprise within a total allocation to the ministry and industrial association. The residual profit is not at the disposal of the enterprise for self-financed investment for, here again, the proportion to be retained by any enterprise will be determined for each individual concern; to meet the complaints of enterprises—as everywhere in eastern Europe under the directive system—that profits earned by virtue of their own economies were immediately confiscated, precluding self-finance planning from one year to the next, the proportion to be retained by each enterprise is fixed, under the reform decree of October 1965, 'for not less than two years'. This concession was extended with effect from the 1970 Plan. The profit retention rate is guaranteed for five years, although in some branches the commitment by the association may be limited to two or three years.

The widely advocated principle of determining directives for a number of years (*kilkoletni*) is intended to reduce arbitrary interference each year by the industrial association. Failure, however, seems to have attended the attempt to reduce to five the indicators given by the latter to the enterprise for constructing the plans for 1970 and 1971–5. One quarter of the drafts submitted were rejected by the associations. The mechanism to operate for the five-year plan period is likely to comprise a broad spectrum of indicators, and regulations enacted in 1969 increased the relative strength of the association over capital formation. In addition to the 'technical development', the association will be entrusted with a 'reserve fund', constituted by the Ministry of Finance from an allocation of one-fifth of planned investment outlay. For the five-year plan, industry has been divided into branches for rapid development, those for moderate growth and those expected to be stationary, in accordance with which each association is being set investment limits (for 1971–3 in the case of the first group, since needs may have to be reconsidered in the last two years of the plan, and for the quinquennium for the two other groups). Any single project will, however, be guaranteed its bank credit for the entire construction period. The new procedure is intended to counter the interruption of building work by annual re-planning while another provision (that any excess outlay is debited to the association's aggregate investment limit and subject to a higher rate) militates against the inflation of building cost.

Experiments in self-financing, initiated four years previously, were extended to all state enterprises in GDR industry in January 1968. Depreciation charges have, from that date, been retained by the enterprise (the precise sums being laid down for the first time in the annual plan for 1968), which retains all profit remaining after payment to specified funds. A capital charge is embodied in the 'production-fund levy' (*Produktionsfondsabgabe*), a tax on profits in proportion to fixed assets and working capital: the rate varies between each branch of industry, with a minimum rate of 5, and a maximum of 20 per cent, the levy being payable to the Ministry of Finance. Investment and premia are covered from the residual profit (*Restgewinn*), the plan for which is calculated on the expectation of a 'normally-operating enterprise'. If an enterprise does not earn enough profit to pay the production-fund levy, the VVB must transfer to that enterprise enough to establish each year a minimum premium fund. In most cases the VVB should obtain the difference from the profit of its other plants, but if no such profits are available for transfer (because each other enterprise is entitled to its own minimum premium fund), the VVB has to obtain a bank loan (at a punitively high rate of interest). The premium fund, thus supplied from profits, must represent at a minimum $1\frac{1}{2}$ per cent of the wage-bill, and $4\frac{1}{2}$ per cent as a maximum; the premium fund is divided into two, one part for managerial staff (the release of which must be ratified by the VVB in an assessment of the efficiency of management), the other for all other workers (payment from which depends upon the actual performance of each).

The VVB annually establishes a planned profit for each of its enterprises; an enterprise which believes that it can earn a higher profit may declare this at the beginning of the year, and 70 per cent of such over-plan profits (within a limit of up to 9 per cent of the wage-bill), is paid into the premium fund. If the enterprise does not declare an above-plan profit, only 30 per cent of any surplus may be attributed to the premium fund; the same limit of 30 per cent applies to profit exceeding the declared above-plan sum. The arrangements on profit-declaration are intended to encourage enterprises to make their financial situation clear and to facilitate accurate macro-economic projections by the Ministry of Finance.

The VVB can, as in Poland, constitute a profit pool from its enterprises; secondly, it makes a levy on them for a 'technology fund' to finance branch-wide research, and thirdly it lays down its own premium fund for rewarding the execution of agreed tasks. This 'disposable fund' (*Verfügungsfonds*) is exacted from enterprises according to a fixed scale; the VVB rewards enterprises from this fund when certain negotiated tasks are fulfilled. Such tasks are agreed between the VVB and an enterprise on a voluntary basis, and the rewards are considerable. The enterprise director may personally receive up to 5000 M, but the premia are mainly intended to recompense a broader stratum of staff: the agreement with the VVB lays down by name the staff to be rewarded for the completion of any specific task (e.g. those in the design office for the elaboration of a new product or process, or a specified workshop brigade for the execution of some production job on time).

New investment regulations of December 1967 and the extension of self-financing arrangements in January 1968 allow, respectively, considerably greater latitude to the enterprise on the size and timing of new construction and authorise enterprises to accumulate profits earned in previous years for capital formation. In step with increasing self-finance, further bank credit (see page 130) is being made available.

RUMANIA

The measures of Rumanian economic reform were, according to resolutions of the Communist Party (at a meeting of the Central Committee in October, and at a National Conference in December 1967), to be enacted before the end of 1969, but this date was postponed for a year, according to an announcement of December 1968. The new financial dispositions unlike those of any other country's reform, include no charge on capital, but the regulations for 1970 go a little further than was envisaged in 1967. While much investment is to remain by non-reimbursable grants from the Ministry of Finance, credit from the banking system will not only, as before, be available for small-scale modernisation but for bigger projects requiring up to 6 years for repayment: depreciation charges remain subject to the disposition of the industrial ministry. As already indicated (page 95), the major development is the establishment of industrial associations; they are to be responsible for the investment plans of constituent enterprises but do not determine their wage bills (although the central planning authorities would retain the right to decide a permitted increment in average wages).

The changes in financial dispositions, already in use in experimenting enterprises and which will be part of the general reform, concern a revision of the premium system (October 1967), involving the liquidation of the 'director's fund', of depreciation charges (December 1968) and of profit allocation (August 1969). The average premium previously paid has been incorporated into wages and salaries and nothing is allowed as premia when no more than the planned profit is earned. But 50 per cent of over-plan profits, if earned by the enterprise's 'own efforts', are attributed to premia, which are now also given to operatives as well as to managerial and technical staff. Payment of these premia (termed *gratificaţii*) is subject to over-fulfilment by the enterprise of the indicator of the ratio of profit to the value of commodities sold and paid for; one-fifth of the anticipated premium can be given out in the course of the year but the remainder is distributed only after the annual accounts have been made up. A second type of premium, termed the 'exceptional fund' is allowed at the discretion of the industrial associations to meritorious individuals or enterprises, but the total may not exceed 3 per cent of the wage-bill in any one enterprise. In the first year of application to experimenting enterprises, the actual 'exceptional fund' was 1 per cent of the wage-bill. Supplementary premia can also be paid from any above-plan *Preisausgleich* (see page 79), gained from selling exports more profitably than planned. There is no evidence that the boards of management, created in all Rumanian industrial enterprises under a decree of April 1969, will have authority over the distribution of premia, although they are empowered to decide upon the elaboration and application of working norms for all categories of staff.

The new regulations on depreciation mark a break with the past in incorporating the allowance for capital repair in the cost of production, instead of in the depreciation charge; the charge, as calculated from January 1969, is consequently a true amortisation allowance. From 1969, 60 per cent of that allowance is paid over to the Ministry of Finance as a source of centralised investment funds, 25 per cent is left at the disposition of the enterprise concerned and 15 per cent will be paid to the association when established (subject to its expenditure solely within the association's enterprises) or, *ad interim*, to the appropriate central administration of the industrial ministry. Regulations provide that any non-expenditure of the fund for capital repair from the planned cost of production may not be counted as an over-fulfilment of planned profit for the purpose of computing the payment to the premium fund.

The regulations promulgated in August 1969 for use in 1970 are avowedly intended to relate, though far from exclusively, the funds that the enterprise can invest to its profit. The profits tax will continue to be determined separately for each enterprise by the Ministry of Finance and the rules lay down that this must not fall below 10 per cent. After payment of tax the first obligation is the repayment of mature bank loans, but minimal retention rates for planned profit are thereafter guaranteed. Some or even all of the residual of planned profit may, however, be taken over by the industrial association if the latter has investment projects (approved by the supervising ministry) which exceed the funds at its disposal from its share of depreciation charges and any other source. While this leaves up to 90 per cent of over-plan profit for the use of the enterprise (as the Ministry decides), the association may also levy up to 3 per cent of total profit (planned and over-plan) 'for work within the association of an urgent nature, but which has not been provided for in the central investment plan'. The aggregate of this levy for industry as a whole may not, however, exceed 2 per cent of total profits earned, and requests to make such imposts will be dealt with by supervising ministries, which will have been allocated appropriate quotas.

The association, furthermore, can take some of the residual of planned profit (after settlement of the other regulated shares therein), to furnish with working or fixed capital any of its enterprises which are making a loss. An official commentary to the regulations states that such transfers must 'concern as few enterprises as possible' and that the Ministry of Finance and the State Planning Committee must receive regular reports on the steps taken towards solvency.

ALBANIA

Addressing the Fifth Party Congress (1966) the Chairman of the Albanian Council of Ministers not only reaffirmed the limited decentralisation of planning decreed earlier in the year (page 96) but added that his government was 'exploiting market relations and other economic instruments more effectively'. Describing the implementation of the changes a year later (to the Fourth Congress of the Democratic Front), the Party First Secretary regretted that 'lower and middle levels' of the economic administration were not taking up their new powers, and it may be that his contemporary, and subsequent, denunciations of devolution in eastern Europe as 'revisionist' have held back response in initiative. An article in the Party journal in June 1969 went so far as to describe the very limited Soviet use of the profit motive as the 'restoration of capitalism'. This reaction is perhaps understandable in the light of the absence of financial autonomy in the Albanian enterprise. Each year it submits to the Ministry of Finance in considerable detail a draft financial plan through the Ministry of Industry and Mining (if it is one of the hundred or so 'national' enterprises), or through its local (*rreth*) Executive Committee. The first ratifies the overall plans of the Ministry and of each local authority for turnover tax and profit deduction. Of planned profit a share (not less than 10 per cent) determined annually for each enterprise is taxed to the Ministry of Finance and a further proportion (between 4 and 10 per cent) is transferred to the enterprise's 'director's fund'. The residual is allocated by the supervising authority (Ministry of Industry or *rreth* council) between fixed investment and working capital according to its investment plan. Of profits earned above plan 30 to 50 per cent is allotted to the 'director's fund', a small amount is set aside as prizes in 'Socialist emulation' (see page 153), 25 per cent goes to the supervising authority (entitled, where appropriate, the 'Ministry fund'), and an allowance is made for staff dwelling-construction by the enterprise; the residual is surrendered as tax.

The director's fund is spent at enterprise discretion on small productive investment, on dwellings and other projects for employee welfare and on managerial premia and staff bonuses. The manner of expenditure of depreciation allowances is laid down by the Ministry of Finance in the investment plan for each supervising authority. Initially drawn up by the State Planning Commission as allocations of equipment and of building work and materials, the investment plan is converted by the Ministry into money terms, the appropriate drawing account for which is then opened at the State Bank. This may be supplemented by small loans for investment outside the financial plan. For current operations managerial premia are payable on fulfilment of plans for global output, product-mix, quality norms and labour productivity.

Autonomous finance

Bulgaria—in April 1966—was the first to launch a reform geared towards a guided market and in elaborating the details drew heavily upon the contemporary discussions in Prague which eventuated in the Czechoslovak reform of January 1967. Although its business relations—including joint companies—have been strongest with Hungary, it did not, later, follow the further-reaching Hungarian devolution. It only tentatively and partially adopted the two governments' undertakings to assure stability to the enterprise during the initial period (the 'normatives' described just below), and has, in fact, altered—though not substantially—the rules governing the disposition of gross revenue five times during 1966–9.

Bulgarian enterprises pay a tax on all fixed and working capital in respect of which credit has been completely repaid, or which had been financed by non-reimbursable subsidy from the Ministry of Finance. In principle the levy is uniform throughout industry—5 per cent of the value of assets payable from gross revenue—but in certain cases a low rate of 2 per cent is payable and a few enterprises are exempt. The second call on gross revenue is a levy (of between 3 and 5 per cent) for the 'fund of technical development', into which the enterprise (here following the Soviet economic reform) also pays 70 per cent of depreciation charges (the remainder of which are transferred to the Ministry of Finance). The part of gross revenue remaining after these two payments is subject to a progressive income tax; wages and expenditure on collective social amenities are paid from the post-tax residual, termed 'income for consumption'.

Not all this 'income for consumption' is necessarily distributed to such outlays, because 'normatives' are prescribed for such allocation; that part of income which cannot be distributed is placed in a 'reserve fund' (a feature of the Hungarian reform). The 'normatives' are a compromise between enterprise autonomy and central direction which is distinctive to present Bulgarian practice. They are determined for the five-year period already mentioned and relate the growth of output per worker (gross revenue after tax per employee), with 'income for consumption' also expressed per employee. For each 10 per cent increase in output per man a smaller increment in 'income for consumption' is authorised. The latter figure varies from industry to industry, but generally does not exceed 3 per cent for the first 10 per cent increase in output per man; the percentage rises with each successive 10 per cent increment in output per man, but at no point does the scale allow for an equivalent 10 per cent increase in the 'income for consumption'. The enterprise can progressively remunerate higher labour productivity, but the latter invariably outstrips the authorised allotment to wages.

Of the 'income for consumption' a percentage fixed by the industrial association is allocated respectively to the premium fund for management and technical staff, and to the bonus fund for workers. The premium fund may be paid out to recipients only when specified compulsory plan indicators have been achieved, the release being decided by the industrial association. The detailed list of recipients and the share in such additional remuneration are determined by the 'economical committee' of each enterprise (see page 151) with respect both to the premium fund for management and the bonus fund for workers. The committee's competence is, however, limited by a minimum rate (as percentage of gross revenue) determined by the industrial association and a maximum that aggregate payments should not exceed 30 per cent of the wage-bill. A set of rules prescribes that the work-team be paid premia in preference to, but not to the exclusion of, the individual workers. The relatively small allotment from post-tax gross revenue to the technical development fund implies that most enterprises will have some recourse to bank credit for net investment, or turn to their industrial association, which runs a pooled fund for technical improvement financed by a levy on constituents.

As a further element of compromise between the former

system and the Czechoslovak and Hungarian models, large investments continue to be financed by Ministry of Finance grant paid through the Industrial Bank, non-reimbursable and bearing no interest. Furthermore bank credit, increasingly seen as a source for enterprise investment, bears a low rate of interest (2 per cent): repayment is, of course, required and when an enterprise does not reimburse on time a higher rate is charged, increasing over six months by steps of 4, 5 and 6 to 8 per cent. In order to discourage an enterprise from accepting this penalty rate of interest, one-fifth of payments under the excess rate is deducted from the premium fund of the enterprise. During the transitional period (originally 1966–8 but since extended) when not all enterprises were operating under the new system and before wholesale prices had been reformed, a 'temporary regulation tax' was levied on enterprises individually in order to offset windfall profits arising from the irrationalities of price relationships. During those years it became apparent that the temporary tax had borne too lightly on certain of the better-equipped enterprises in an industry, or between industries in relation to gross revenue earned from sales at the ruling wholesale prices: as a consequence, enterprises which were less well-equipped, or in industries generally disadvantaged by price in relation to cost, lost workers who moved to higher-wage enterprises.

The use of gross revenue is one of the two main features—the other being determination to introduce domestic competition—linking Bulgaria with the 1967 changes in Czechoslovakia, where, however, dispositions now chiefly relate to profit, as is the case in Hungary.

CZECHOSLOVAKIA

The first charge on gross revenue or profit in a Czechoslovak enterprise is the tax on capital. In 1967–9 enterprises paid a higher rate of tax on installed fixed assets (6 per cent) than on working capital (2 per cent) but in 1970 both are charged at 6 per cent; the rate is uniform throughout industry although some exemptions have been made in other sectors (domestic trade and, temporarily, for some municipal services). New fixed capital financed by borrowing from the banking system will not be subject to the levy, but bank interest has tended to be a little higher than the levy: although it is currently the same as the levy with respect to fixed capital, it was originally 8 per cent (in 1966) and on working capital 4 per cent (6 per cent in 1966). Some preferentially low rates of interest are available on fixed capital borrowed for projects in less-developed regions and for working capital in domestic trade.

The second, and heavier, tax on the enterprise is that on gross revenue (in 1967 and 1968) and on profits (from late 1968). It was set in 1967 at a rate of 18 per cent in industry and in construction (other rates included 30 per cent on centrally-run domestic trade enterprises, 16 per cent in local-authority enterprises and in autonomously-financed drafting agencies and 8 per cent in the tourist industry). Only minor changes were made at the beginning of 1968 but in October a tax on profit was introduced which gradually replaced the tax on gross revenue. It applied to all industrial, construction and foreign-trade firms from January 1970. The change was occasioned by the high profits being earned as a result of the exaggeration of costs underlying the new price lists (see page 78). Liability as profit is computed after payment of the charge on assets and the tax at 65 per cent is linear.

After a disappointing experience in 1966, using the Hungarian practice (applied since 1957) of limiting the mean wage per man to a specified increase over the average in the preceding year, a wage-tax was imposed in 1967, under which the tax rate rose in sharp progression as the total wage-bill exceeded that paid out in the previous year: the tax rate was 100 per cent of the increment over the previous year's wage-bill when the increase reached 8 per cent. In the event, these punitive tax rates were not enough to deter enterprises from heavy increases in wages (as the tightness of the labour market justified) and during 1967–8 tax was incurred when the increase in the average wage-bill exceeded the increment in labour productivity (initially on a scale permitting a 3·4 per cent increase in wages when a 5 per cent productivity increment was reached, but subsequently lowering the upper limits to 2·9 per cent of wage rise released by a 4·5 per cent growth of productivity). Liability to the wage-tax in 1969 was assessed on either of two conditions—when the rate of growth of the mean wage in the enterprise exceeded a rate equal to the expected rate of growth of net national product or when the enterprise raised its average employment. It was further altered in 1970: a flat 25 per cent was levied as a new contribution to financing health and social security and progression thereafter related to any increment in the average wage.

The Czechoslovak government, like the Hungarian, began its two reforms by pledging stability of tax rates. In the Czechoslovak reform of 1958, 'normatives' were given for five years to each enterprise—on the part of profit to be retained, on average earnings in a ratio to productivity and rates at which payments could be made to incentive funds. The stability lasted only two years before discretionary assessment was reimposed. The commitment of 1967—that tax rates on profit would not be altered by more than one per cent a year during the initial phase—lasted no longer, but a new—though quantitatively smaller—guarantee was offered for 1970 that no taxation should exceed 85 per cent of profit.

HUNGARY

The Hungarian government undertook in 1968 not to amend tax rates nor profit-distribution rules for three years (though incorporating in advance systematic but marginal changes for each year). No alterations were made in the first two years but it seemed likely that the formula penalising increments in the average wage of an enterprise (see below) would have to be related to the wage-bill in 1970 because of tension in a strained labour market as enterprises sought to recruit low-wage staff in order to pay its existing workers more.

Current Hungarian legislation provides for a uniform tax of 5 per cent, payable from profits, on all fixed and working capital, with some trivial exemptions for certain small industries and a few low-profit or deficitary enterprises. For the first year of the reform working capital financed under an outstanding bank loan was exempt from the tax, but this exemption was withdrawn in 1969. As in Czechoslovakia, the rate of interest is greater than the rate of tax—8 per cent on medium-term loans and 7 per cent on long-term loans—although lower, preferential rates are allowed by the banking system for investments likely to benefit exports for convertible currencies, in specified under-developed regions (a facility withdrawn in 1969), or in certain services. Profit remaining after the capital tax is divided into three parts; after a 10 per cent allocation to a 'reserve fund' the residual is allocated to a 'development fund' and a 'sharing fund'. Counting assets as fixed and working capital, the ratio of asset value to the aggregate of assets plus the wage-bill is the fraction applied to profits to derive the allocation to the 'development fund'; in aggregating the wage-bill with assets, the standard procedure is to give the former double weight, but this co-efficient of two is not entirely uniform, varying in a few industries and in a number of other sectors from as much as eight to 0·6. The fraction applied to profit to determine the 'sharing fund' is the ratio of the wage-bill to the aggregate of the wage-bill plus assets; the same co-efficient, normally two, but changing as for the previous calculation by industry, is applied to wages in determining the aggregate.

Taxation of each fund is applied at the next stage. No tax is borne by the reserve fund; a flat 60 per cent rate is applied to the development fund, leaving 40 per cent at the disposal of the enterprise for investment; the 'industrial rate' of 60 per cent applies also to construction and transport but a lower rate of 45 per cent is applied to agricultural enterprises and a higher rate to trade (70 per cent). Tax on the sharing fund is both steeply progressive on the allocation in any one year and discriminates against increases in the average wage over that in the base year, 1967. The progressive element is related to the proportion which the sharing fund bears to the wage-bill; that part of the sharing fund which does not exceed 3 per cent of the wage-bill goes untaxed, but thereafter the tax rate increases with each percentage equivalent in terms of the wage-bill until the maximum tax rate of 70 per cent is applied to that part of the sharing fund which exceeds 13 per cent of the wage-bill; after deduction of taxes at these rates, a further deduction is made of any excess of the actually-paid average wage over the average wage paid in 1967 multiplied by the number of workers. Provision was made in advance for the three-year period that the tax on the sharing fund would fall successively in 1969 and 1970.

The development fund serves, as its name implies, for enterprise investment; for the first year, 1968, a limit was imposed on the proportion of that fund at enterprise disposal which could be spent on workers' housing, but this constraint was lifted in 1969. The development fund is also the recipient of that portion of depreciation charges authorised for enterprise retention: in general, 60 per cent remains for the enterprise, with the remaining 40 per cent paid to the Ministry of Finance; the share of depreciation retained is somewhat reduced when enterprises have made major investments during the preceding four years on the ground that straight-line depreciations involve the accrual of funds long before expenditure or renewals. Capital repairs were, as in other eastern European countries, considered as a supplement to the depreciation charge proper, but since 1966 they have been counted as a component of production costs. Since 1959, when wholesale prices were first reformed, that capital-repair component had been left at the disposal of the enterprise and —because the depreciation charge exceeded that justified by straight-line computation—tacitly allowed a charge to be made on capital. This dissimulation may be attributed to the narrow interpretation of Marx's labour theory of value then prevailing, which opposed the propriety of levying interest on socialist enterprises. In the 1968 price reform such disguise was no longer needed and depreciation charges have been reduced to standard form.

By 1969 half industrial investment was being executed by enterprises and the draft of the five-year plan (as yet unratified by parliament or Party) provided for the reduction of centralised investment to 28 per cent by 1975. In 1968, 12 per cent of investment was financed by bank loans—a proportion that was to be at least doubled by the end of the quinquennium. Serious consideration was being given to the creation of an institution outside the banking system which could mobilise enterprise, and perhaps private, savings for capital which could be used, *inter alia*, to facilitate new entry into monopolised sectors.

Access to bank funds

When thoughts are turning in Hungary towards a state-controlled stock market, the earlier ideological restrictions on the use of banking seem far past. Although the prohibition of mercantile credit—indebtedness between enterprises—remains, so that any loans must be made by a bank, the banking system is no longer a mere post-office for the Ministry of Finance. Inevitably the changes have gone furthest in the states adopting the guided market principle.

The guarantees of the Czechoslovak and Hungarian governments on stable tax rates affecting the enterprise emphatically do not apply to rates of interest charged by the banking system, which is thereby enabled—in accordance with the annual plan (respectively, the 'Economic Directives' or the 'Directives on Credit Policy')—to adjust its rates as economic conditions require. Rates are not, however, intended to vary within any one calendar (i.e. planning) year.

For eastern Europe as a whole the implication of economic reform for the banking system has been threefold. First, as already indicated in the context of enterprise dispositions, non-reimbursable investment grants are being replaced by bank loans; banks are being required, secondly, to filter applications for capital finance, and, thirdly, to pay interest on enterprises' deposits when such accounts are subject, like the rest of the working capital, to the tax on capital holdings.

The Yugoslav banking law of 1965 offers a model to which the more advanced reforms are likely to tend. It became no longer necessary for socialist enterprises (those operated by workers' management) to hold their accounts with the state banking system, which had been the main instrument of central control and inspection after the dismantling in 1952 of Soviet-type central planning; from 1965 when a second major phase of economic reform had definitively converted Yugoslavia to a market economy, bank controls were abolished and competition permitted among banks; enterprises were authorised to buy shares in banks, and limitations to the creation of new banks (subject to normal financial guarantees) were removed. In Hungary and Czechoslovakia the abolition of directives to enterprises removed the mainstay of the former banking practice, i.e. to supplement and verify the implementation by enterprises of centrally-determined plans for production, sales and investment, Although beginning to be discussed in the guided market economies, no element of competition between banks has been introduced.

There has been a clear trend to create new banks which can give specific attention to enterprises operating under the reformed procedures. In Bulgaria the Investitsionna Banka was merged with the central bank in early 1967 and in mid-1968 specialist banks were created to serve the needs of state enterprises both for short- and long-term investment: one was created for industry, construction and transport and another for agriculture, domestic trade and public services. In the GDR the first stage in the bank reform was the creation in 1964 of Industrie-Bankfilialen as branches of the Noten-bank, each devoted to a specific branch of industry (up to, but no more than, three VVBs). The Investitionbank was dissolved when a specific industrial bank was established in 1968, to take as customers all VVB-administered enterprises in industry and trade; as already mentioned (page 39) a special bank had existed for small-scale industry and there had, in addition, always been a specialist banking service for agriculture.

The stage of the Rumanian reform introduced in the regulations for the 1970 Plan widened the functions of the Banca de Investiții. Its authority to grant small 'modernisation loans' to enterprises has, as mentioned above, been extended to provide for projects repayment which will take as long as six years, and it can choose recipients according to their expected efficiency. Banking inspection is required as a condition of the provision of credit for working capital, for which each enterprise will have a 'normative'—to be established yearly and with no guarantee of stability. Bank managers are enjoined to verify that no over-plan inventories are financed on credit. A profitable enterprise can escape such bank control to the extent that it is allowed to build up working capital from profits (although this is subject to the proportion of planned profit surrendered to the Ministry of Finance at the latter's discretion). For the bulk of industrial investment, the banking system remains merely a channel for administering budget grants, not, from 1970, distributing them to enterprises, but only to associations.

As part of the reform, the banking system was rearranged in 1968. The extreme centralisation of the Banca de Stat (which reverted to its pre-nationalisation title, Banca Naţională, in 1965) was eased by the creation of a bank for agriculture (its predecessor having been liquidated in 1960) and of another for foreign trade.

The Rumanian credit system nevertheless has been rather more flexible in the past than in other east European countries.

Following a credit reform in 1959, ministries and their central administrations were authorised to create their own reserve fund (originally constituted by a levy of 13 per cent of reserves of the enterprises under their control); these funds escaped central bank control, the remainder of which was virtually eliminated so far as industrial enterprises were concerned by a simultaneous requirement that enterprises participate directly in the preparation of the Bank's quarterly credit plan. Furthermore, a great deal of consumer credit bypasses the banking system (as also in Bulgaria) through mutual-credit unions organised for the staff of almost any enterprise and state institution. Because, however, the Rumanian enterprise was not freed from the subordination to the industrial ministry when the 1959 credit reform took place, its financial independence was more a convenience to the director than an expression of any genuine autonomy.

A second general tendency is the direction of enterprises to use the banking system as direct commercial clients for both short- and long-term loans.

In Bulgaria bank credit for both terms remains centrally allocated each year by industry: within the limits of each quota for a given industry, however, the banks select those projects which appear to them to be most profitable with respect to long- and medium-term investments. No allocation by branch is, however, made for working capital: the availability of this credit depends in part upon the liquidity of the relevant bank, for it attracts deposits from enterprises at an appropriate rate of interest. The further decision of July 1968 on the economic reform observed that a more flexible interest-rate policy was desirable: the schedule of interest-rates had, in fact, been revised late the previous year. Following the arrangement described below in the GDR, the Bulgarian National Bank has begun to establish branches at the head office of each industrial association.

In Hungary banks are also in principle dependent upon enterprise deposits of funds in interest-bearing accounts for the supply of credit at their disposal and, as already indicated, interest rates may be changed at short notice. In neither country, however, does there appear to be any requirement by the government (or by the central bank in relation to the other banks) that deposits bear any specified relationship to loans and advances. In both countries and in Czechoslovakia certain large investments continue to be financed by public, non-reimbursable grants, and aggregate credit policy remains in the hands of the central authorities. In Hungary a Credit Policy Council, of which the chairman is the President of the National Bank, issues the annual 'Directives on Credit Policy', but within those instructions the Hungarian National Bank has more executive autonomy than any other central Bank in east Europe. For Bulgaria and Czechoslovakia the Ministry of Finance establishes an investment plan by industry which sets out quotas for bank credit on the basis of likely profitability within each given industry. Central constraints on the banks' choice of client weigh a little less heavily in Czechoslovakia than in Bulgaria for, if too few creditworthy clients for fixed investment present themselves in any one industry in relation to the investment-plan quota, the bank may reallocate the unspent credit to suitable clients in other sectors. Repayment periods vary from industry to industry, but the interest rate is uniform (with the minor exceptions noted on page 121). In 1969 some, and in 1970 all, Czechoslovak enterprises were required to rely on their own working capital; until the 1967 reform they had virtually been guaranteed what funds they needed by the State Bank, but in 1967–8 any increment over the 1966 level had to be financed—save in exceptional circumstances—from gross revenue.

Superficially, the increase in bank-finance of investment in Poland, since the second stage of the economic reform introduced in 1966, is similar to that in Bulgaria, Czechoslovakia and Hungary. Priority projects remain financed by non-reimbursable grant but the share of bank credit in capital formation is already substantial. It is a necessary corollary to the continued imposition of investment limits upon the Polish enterprise, however, that the banks no more than channel funds to the projects approved in the annual plan.

In the GDR the deliberately intimate relations between the Industrie-Bankfilialen (first of the Notenbank and now of the Bank für Industrie und Handel) and the VVB blur the respective responsibilities on project selection between bank and industrial association, and may even allow loan allotments by branch of industry for fixed investment to be decided within the banking system, rather than by the central planning authorities (which, nevertheless, retain control of last resort). The allocation of short-term credit by branch (and therefore by VVB) is entirely in the hands of the Notenbank, which need only have its annual aggregate credit plan approved by the Council of Ministers: not only do the VVBs draft their own quarterly plans for credit (the eventual actual distribution emerging in negotiation), but each credit plan, when approved, includes a reserve fund (rather as in Rumania) at the disposition of the VVB, which may be used for lending to enterprises needing funds in excess of plan.

Because all long-term investment for which an enterprise requires outside resources is still to be by non-reimbursable grant, the Rumanian banking system has few new responsibilities under the reform. The Investment Bank remains in this sphere no more than the agent of the Ministry of Finance, but its authority to grant medium-term loans allows it some discretion. Industrial associations take a proportion of the profits of enterprises to re-invest in enterprises within the group; this form of self-finance within the association is, however, estimated in advance and classified with grants from the Ministry of Finance in the annual plan for investment by branch of industry. The association can, as already mentioned, deduct up to 2 per cent of the profits of its enterprises to constitute a fund for medium-term investments in excess of this plan.

The Albanian State Bank remains an agent of the Ministry of Finance for fixed investment, but the enterprise usually has enough working capital of its own. The Bank can supplement either fund at a 2 per cent rate of interest.

9
Managers and Workers

ECONOMIC REFORM, with varying degrees of devolution, leaves an open question on the nature of the state enterprise in eastern Europe. Under the directive system, the subdivision of the industrial process has been made on technological grounds, subject to the administrative requirement that industrial ministries were horizontal combinations. The few exceptions to this pattern for the ministry were made when industry processed an agricultural product (forestry and the timber industry have a common ministry in Bulgaria, Poland and Rumania, and agriculture and food-processing are linked in Bulgaria, Hungary and Poland); some ministries are also broad enough to be considered a vertical combination (fuel and power in Bulgaria, mining and metallurgy in the GDR, metallurgy and engineering in Hungary and mining and power in Poland). The division of industrial ministries into 'central administrations', to which compulsory industrial associations still tend to correspond, much reduced in practice the composition of enterprises by vertical integration. While those associations as a general rule have been horizontal combinations, most of the trusts retained in Hungary and some of the central offices newly established in Rumania are vertical.

Within the horizontal associations or their predecessors, the scale and product-mix of the enterprise tended to be defined strictly by the technological process, although for historical reasons a few concerns, which before nationalisation had spanned a rather broader range of products, were retained as single enterprises. Enterprise autonomy within the guided market has raised the possibility that an enterprise may diversify into other products in the same industry, duplicate the facilities formerly offered by its suppliers or recipients in vertical extensions, or merge with others either horizontally or vertically. It may be relevant that these powers have long been available to Yugoslav enterprises, but have not greatly been used; in Hungary, however, it is now open to an enterprise to develop 'complementary activities' at its discretion and to pool resources with others to establish 'common enterprises'.

The creation of an enterprise has hitherto been by administrative order, and the new laws on the enterprise, enacted in Hungary and abortively drafted in Czechoslovakia, continue to reserve the power of establishment, separation and liquidation to the legal founder, a government Minister or local authority.

The sole significant case where a conspicuous divorce has been demanded is that by the Škoda engineering concern in Pilsen from the motor-car works of the same name in Mlada Boleslav, on the grounds that the poor quality of cars manufactured by the latter has brought its machinery into disrepute.

De-concentration in the interests of greater domestic competition (see page 99) may be imposed by government decision but, generally, against the pressures of the enterprises concerned and the technical efficiency of large units. The shortage of competent managers is still acute: the old managerial class (proprietors, bank delegates and managing directors), which ran an industry much smaller than that of today, was largely destroyed. Two decades later there are few left from senior positions in that period in active life, and the concentration of scarce managerial talent is an argument for maintaining industrial associations. The businessman with the greatest personal span of effective control in eastern Europe is the director-general of a VVB in the GDR; the one with the least is the manager of any Albanian plant who, according to a decree of 1968, must frequently change his post, lest he succumb to 'bureaucratic tendencies', and subject himself to self-criticism when so required by 'working-class control'.

There is no enterprise in eastern Europe too large for one

director to manage: sub-division of the enterprise is scarcely required for management efficiency, although the practice, well established before the war, of appointing a director-general, delegating authority to a number of managers, has been continued for large plants. Such managers, like other staff, are subordinate to the single head of the enterprise, following the principle of line management (see page 29). The only deliberate exception towards functional management seems to be an experiment introduced in Rumania in late 1968: evoking the ideology of 'collectivism', the government has authorised the appointment of sub-managers for individual departments who, in defined cases, will be responsible not to the director-general but to the board of management (described on page 151).

Enterprise objectives

The communist parties introducing the directive system readily embraced the view that the goal of a socialist enterprise would be to generate marxian use value, rather than exchange value: 'production for satisfaction of needs would replace production for profit'. The eastern European national plan was considered a representation of social desiderata, and the only operational requirement of an implementing enterprise was hence 'to fulfil and over-fulfil the plan'. As political rethinking paralleled economic devolution—demonstrated in Hungary and Poland in 1956—the distinction came to be appreciated between the ideal goal of a socialist enterprise and the effective goal of the manager, namely, the maximisation of bonuses within his preferred volume of effort and time. While not altogether abandoning the honourable idylls of the 'collective' and 'socialist emulation' as a moral belief, the official portrayal of the enterprise has come to include conflict, which could be both external (between the enterprise and the interests of society as a whole, of other enterprises and of consumers), and internal (between management and staff and between different groups of employees).

The state enterprise in eastern Europe has authority over

fewer of its activities than a typical capitalist concern, although under either social form some economic events within the enterprise are consequences of external decisions. It is a matter for further study whether the sphere of authority of the eastern European enterprise is subject to greater variation. Certainly in the Western mixed economy the form of government regulation changes relatively slowly; but it is possible that internal reorganisation and mergers with, or separation from, other firms tend to be less abrupt or disruptive than the rapid increments, diminutions and amendments to the administrative orders binding the socialist enterprise in eastern Europe. Plans for stabilising the constraints imposed upon the enterprise and government responses are nevertheless evocative: they include the reiterated demands for a multi-year plan indicator in Poland, the broken promise in Czechoslovakia in 1958 that profit-deduction ratios on any enterprise would be fixed for five years and the limitation in the eventual reform of 1967 of tax changes to a maximum of 1 per cent per year on enterprise income, the invariability of profit-distribution formulae in Hungary for three years from 1968 and the concession of five-year 'normatives' in the Bulgarian reform. The right of the central authorities or industrial associations annually (or even monthly) to vary the enterprise's sphere of control undermines any endeavour to formulate a precise economic calculus of enterprise behaviour. The problem is evidently that of interlocking two distinct management mechanisms, one under which some enterprise decisions are governed (or influenced) by parameters (prices, wages, rates of interest or of taxation) and others by the direct orders of higher authority.

Where the difficulties of co-ordinating the two mechanisms are being put aside, as prospectively in Czechoslovakia and actually in Hungary, by the concentration of all information from the central authorities into parameters (some generated by a self-regulating market), the further problem is set of the ultimate responsibility of the enterprise. The Yugoslav principle of 'self-administration' was chosen as the antithesis to Stalin's politico-economic centralism, although the parallel decentralisation within the Party (which at the same time— 1952—changed itself from the 'Communist Party' to the 'League of Communists') was partially frustrated until 1966 by the centripetal pressure of the security services (UDBA). Private initiative is increasingly being allowed—as it has long been in Yugoslavia—to fill the gaps of the socialist mechanism, or to rescue small enterprises, such as personal services, retailing, restaurants and hotels, from the deficits induced by over-centralisation, but any restoration of a substantial private sector in industry has been firmly checked by the Soviet invasion of Czechoslovakia and the subsequent insistence of the Soviet government on guarantees for the pre-eminence of a socialism of its own definition.

Without, however, yielding means of production to private ownership, the governments embracing guided markets may now choose between 'public' or 'enterprise' property. So far, they have reiterated that enterprises are owned by the state and that the government has the power to require their conformity to its decisions, but the Yugoslav example whereby state property is vested in the enterprise has, at least tacitly, gained recognition by the short-lived existence of boards of management in Czechoslovakia, and by the emergence of limited forms of employee participation in Bulgaria, the GDR, Poland and Rumania, of some external consultation in Hungary and of 'workers' control' in Albania.

Attitudes to the enterprise

Before examining the new institutional form of the enterprise, some reference may be made to the views on the enterprise now being expressed in eastern Europe by lawyers, sociologists, businessmen and economists.

The legal problem of the enterprise resides in the overlap between administrative law and civil law. Except in Albania, where all the relations of an enterprise are held to be within the sphere of administrative law (the standard legal text-book speaks of a socialist industrial enterprise as subject to 'command'), the broad division is between an enterprise's relation with higher authorities, falling within the scope of administrative law, and inter-enterprise actions, which have the character of civil law; relations of an enterprise to its employees are everywhere (Albania included) one of civil law. Czechoslovak and east German law has cut through the problem by formulating a separate branch of 'economic law', but elsewhere—the debate is particularly acute in Poland—the position of inter-enterprise relations is unclear. When, for example, a factory in a country which maintains central allocation of materials is authorised to receive a stated supply, acceptance of its custom by a distribution organisation involves an administrative order (inherent in quantity of products allocated), state standardisation (with respect to the qualities of product), and government regulation (on the price of the material, and on penalties for violation of contract and rules governing resort to arbitration); a legal act ensues between equal entities (in the sense that neither is subject to the authority of either), none of the essential elements of which have been determined by the partners themselves.

The situation has been simplified in countries which have abandoned the directive system, and it is noteworthy that the law on arbitration was revised in Bulgaria, Czechoslovakia and Hungary to correspond with the new autonomy of enterprises. In Rumania, by contrast, cases of dispute between enterprises over supply contracts were transferred in 1969 from the State Arbitration Tribunal to the authority issuing the supply plan concerned.

A sociologist would perhaps go on to say that an exaggerated belief in the efficacy of legal prescriptions in regulating economic activity has led to a degeneration of the management system—first by bureaucratic over-regulation, secondly, by inducing individuals to obey only those legal norms which conform to their personal interest and aspirations, or to pay more attention to countering the acts of their supervising agency than to the substantive task, and, thirdly, by allowing spheres of authority and decision-making either to overlap (and generally to conflict) or to fail to meet (and thereby to create an administrative vacuum). The sociological study of the enterprise, apparently most advanced in Hungary and Poland, has shown how far inquiry still has to go for a proper understanding of staff motivation. One of the analyses now under way is of the point at which a worker ceases to co-operate voluntarily with management by his judgement of comparative working conditions or by a feeling of being 'wronged' (raising, under socialism, Marx's critique of capitalist alienation), and related problems of controlling interpersonal relationships, of engendering technical inventiveness, or of directing employees to maintain mutual control and support (the 'homeostasis' of cybernetics).

An inquiry of the Rumanian Institute of Economic Research in 1967 revealed that managers considered $7\frac{1}{2}$ hours of their working day to be concerned with inessentials, but only one in five felt able to say 'yes' to the question 'Have you ever examined your own use of your time?', and one in two to 'Do you need new techniques of information?' to know what was going on in the factory. They all wanted fewer controls by the ministry: the reply from a Bucharest glassworks observed that there were each day on average two supervisory visitors to the plant.

On the other hand, one in two Polish managers, polled in 1962 by the secretariat of the Economic Council, declared themselves satisfied with most aspects of their jobs, and 59 per cent believed that their post fully used their personal abilities. It might be suggested that some of the satisfied majority would have to vacate their posts if Poland adopted the reforms of Hungary. The disintegration of the Hungarian Party in November 1956 (see page 34), while not relaxing the authority typical of a governing communist party, permitted, in subsequent years, the nomination of managers largely for their technical competence. Managerial ability in that country meets rather higher standards than elsewhere in eastern Europe, where the stricter continuity of party organisation has tended excessively to elevate political loyalty among the criteria for appointment.

The businessmen who write in the press, participate in management or economic-policy conferences, or attend post-experience management courses, declare themselves for the greater part dissatisfied. At a conference in Warsaw on 'Economic Incentives in the Industrial Enterprise' held in 1962, the General Director of the country's largest confectionery works declared that 'as a rule, enterprise management works under conditions which do not conduce to a proper utilisation of qualifications and abilities. The enterprise manager has to devote too much of his time to coping with external difficulties, and too little . . . to the enterprise and its tasks.' He added that many external problems required the personal attention of the director himself because representations had to be made at a high level of the administrative hierarchy, and that the management sphere of authority was so narrowly defined that 'gaining the authority and respect of staff . . . is practically unattainable'. It is doubtless the outstanding managers who express themselves in public, and who are frustrated by an environment hostile to the entrepreneurship they could supply.

When it is the turn of the economist to explain the enterprise, the brief answer is that managers conform by and large to assumptions on behaviour common to those accepted for a market economy: they tend to maximise personal remuneration (through salary, premia or participation in a 'sharing fund'), where the theory of the firm under market conditions expects profit maximisation, but are not, of course, unaffected by considerations of prestige, public recognition and authority. Socialist micro-economics, at the present stages of reform, need much further analysis for a thorough reply, and the interpretations made in this study can only be preliminary.

The manager's strategy

For an enterprise in the guided-market economies of Czechoslovakia and Hungary, the strategy for a manager does not greatly differ from that of his counterpart, the non-shareholding executive, in a standard market economy: the crucial problem lies beyond the ambit of the manager in the nature of the property he controls. So long as it remains a 'state enterprise', the assets are, in principle, subject to whatever compulsions the constituted authorities may require. Only in Yugoslavia does 'enterprise property' furnish a countervailing right of self-determination.

Boards of management in the enterprise and trade unions at the federal level were emerging in Czechoslovakia in 1968 to press alternative economic options upon the manager and government respectively, but the trend has clearly been checked and no corresponding movement can be perceived elsewhere. Hungary is the extreme case of devolution to managerial authority. The official view is that the manager, despite his general competence as an entrepreneur, was until 1968 not only subordinate to directives, but could hide his omissions to act behind an absence of directives. Under the reform, the manager must be both untrammelled by orders from a board within the enterprise and exposed on his own responsibility for not taking any appropriate initiative. By the same token, he should personally reap, and himself determine, the rewards of risk and innovation within government-set limits.

The extent of the initiative of an enterprise in Hungary is exemplified by its power—unique in eastern Europe, though encouraged in Yugoslavia—to establish subsidiaries jointly with others. Profits of such 'common enterprises' (one, Budavox, is the subsidiary of five sponsors, but the number is usually two or three) are divided between it and the sponsors, by predetermined accord on a scale geared to its success. The profits shared out are pooled with those of the sponsors, the 'sharing fund' of which thereby benefits (following the rules described on page 123) without necessarily any work contribution by the staff of the sponsoring enterprise. In fact, if not in form, the latter are deriving income from the capital their enterprise invested from its development fund.

The Hungarian exception is a minor step towards the award of gain or loss from risk-taking which is dissociated from the direct product of labour. Marx's labour theory of value has been interpreted, in east Europe as in the USSR, as permitting the active population to be remunerated solely with respect to personal effort: judging themselves to follow his condemnation of exploitation of workers by land owners and capitalists, the post-war governments have done their best to outlaw 'speculation'. The earning of interest on private deposits in the Savings Bank and rights of inheritance —always permitted—have begun to be extended to enable enterprises to gain interest on their bank deposits, but no debt instruments exist other than cash. The use of such titles, the varying liquidity and risk in which is rewarded by differential (including negative) returns, is the crucial threshold of the market economy which no government is, as yet, prepared to take.

Managerial autonomy and worker participation—discussed further below—limit the return to risk to reflection in current money earnings, an arrangement which has two shortcomings. First, the horizon of the worker with respect to his re-muneration is at most one year (even the distribution of Hungarian 'sharing funds' at an annual interval has caused trouble) and it is not much longer for managers: they do not want to forgo early dividends for a longer maturing innova-tion or initiative. Secondly, the degree of loss borne by the risk-takers, as shown in earnings, has a lower limit in minimal acceptable living standards (the average of which is in any case much lower than in the industrial economies of western Europe) and, for any one enterprise, in the earnings of com-parable occupations with other firms. Yugoslav earnings-differentials are perhaps as wide in this respect as an economy can go with unemployment and a labour surplus in agriculture and in under-developed regions. But the manpower shortages of Czechoslovakia, the GDR and Hungary (and the absence of regional divergences in the two latter) preclude a similar result.

While Hungary has gone at least a little way to reward risk and initiative, their aversion remains a characteristic of the directive system, in which management behaviour when the plan is being built is chiefly influenced by the 'ratchet-principle' (see page 103). Information is distorted by lower levels of the industrial hierarchy in reporting upwards; a process of bargaining takes place between each level; and arbitrary 'corrections' of drafts submitted by lower levels are made by higher authorities (constituting a source of internal inconsistency of the final plan at all levels). Feedback of inconsistent information occurs because, since enterprises may be supplying distorted information, their supervisors react by seeking to redress the degree of unreliability without detailed knowledge of the real potential of the enterprise: the reaction generates unrealistic or internally inconsistent plans which cause enterprises to intensify misinformation as a matter of self-defence.

Superintendents have evolved two methods to interrupt this feedback, by verifying data supplied by enterprises more closely, and by creating incentives for revealing potential at the stage of plan construction. The extreme organisational form of the first reaction was the Czechoslovak merger of the Committee for State Control with the Central Statistical Administration into the State Commission for Peoples' Control and Statistics; the separation of the two bodies and the disappearance of an agency of formal control were concomitants of economic reform. But even where statistical reporting is supervised, the volume of information and the impossibility of detailed authentication constitute a barrier.

In summary, because a manager seeks to maximise bonuses for himself and his staff, plan proposals are submitted in a form influenced by expected conditions of plan fulfilment; within these conditions, a director behaves rationally, and if his behaviour conflicts with the objectives of the central authorities, it is not necessarily he, but the management mechanism, which requires investigation.

At the stage of plan fulfilment, the manager arranges

production to gain the maximum individual and group bonuses consistent with securing a bonus-maximising target in the next round of plan preparation, for too high an over-fulfilment can lead superintendents to raise subsequent-period goals. A clear case of production arrangement to improve bonuses arises in a concentration of output late in the year. This practice can be traced to three causes. First, premia are paid monthly in accordance with the corresponding plan fulfilment. The aim is therefore precisely to meet monthly goals (for what has actually been paid out cannot be revoked from remuneration) while any over-fulfilment should not be squandered before bonuses for each of the preceding eleven months have been settled; under-fulfilment in the final month will not cause the withdrawal of earlier payments.

If an enterprise anticipates that the ministry will augment a production target later in the plan year, it will, for example, delay assembling as many final products as it can. It will thus either have reserves for meeting the increment or may extract additional premia from the industrial association in return for shouldering supplementary tasks; the association in the GDR and Poland has a reserve to pay premia for such purposes.

Finally, because the plan for the subsequent year is based upon the 'probable fulfilment' extrapolated from the showing of the first seven (or at most nine) months, a low output figure for those months is an advantage. The industrial association is aware of the trend likely in the last five (or three) months of the year, but cannot propose a higher estimate to its ministry, lest the upswing should fail to occur. Output of new products is likely to be started sufficiently late in the year for the initial high cost phase to terminate around December: the annual average cost of production will be inflated for the comparison to be made in the subsequent year.

Product-mix plans are imposed by the central authorities to respond to difficulties created by use of a price structure which fails properly to reflect their preferences relative to existing scarcities; where the product-mix is not precisely specified, variation from that envisaged by the plan authority in a goal denominated in value can arise from price differentials and from subcontracting. Since prices in these directive systems are not market-determined, differentials can arise in profitability per unit of wage-bill (which tends to be the limiting factor where, as in Albania, the GDR, Poland and Rumania a wage-bill or cost-of-production target is imposed) for different products or stages of production. Thus in one Polish textile combine a zloty of wages in the cotton mill produces anything from a 0·40 zl. loss to a 3·00 zl. profit depending upon the type of yarn produced; a zloty of wages in the weaving mill can yield a loss of 1·00 zl. or a profit of 0·90 zl.; and in the finishing shop the range is between a 7·00 zl. loss and no less than a 42·00 zl. profit. In such conditions a relatively small manoeuvre of the product-mix towards the more profitable, and less labour-intensive, product makes a substantially better showing on fulfilment of the profitability, labour productivity and output-volume targets. Subcontracting can permit a firm to switch workers and machines towards phases of output which improve its formal performance in the plan indicators.

Risk and innovation are little sought because the manager knows that he is practically never blamed for not doing anything not explicitly required of him; a risk unsuccessfully taken, on the other hand, results in loss of premia for himself and his staff, and, in serious cases, his own demotion. Moreover, if his venture succeeds, his material and moral rewards will be modest relative to the risks incurred. The slow rate of technical progress is a constant complaint of the central authorities, for disincentives to innovate are strong while incentives are weak.

Management training

Two decades of subordination to directives have deterred from entry to senior management the individuals best able to make use of the new potential of economic devolution. Personnel changes have started *pari passu* with reform, but considerable hope is now being placed by government on the retraining of existing managers and on the formation of candidates for senior positions. Management schools have now appeared in all countries except Albania. The oldest appears to be the Polish National Centre for Management Training set up in 1960 (with the help of the International Labour Organisation) but the Institute for the Organisation of the Engineering Industry also in Warsaw, despite its more limited name, carries out management training and research; both are also found in the more strictly academic sphere in the post-experience courses and graduate training of the Central School of Planning and Statistics. An Institute of Management was constituted as a faculty of the Prague High School of Economics in 1965, as soon as reform entered the field of wide public discussion. The ILO has also assisted the foundation in 1967 of the Institute of Management of the Ministry of Labour in Hungary, the National Institute for Management and Organization in Rumania, and the Management Training Centre at the University of Sofia in Bulgaria. In Hungary two other ministries have created their own management centres. Such developments have paralleled those in the USSR: a Management Institute was created in Riga in 1963, and there are now an Inter-faculty Laboratory for Problems of Production Administration in Moscow University, and management departments in the Ordzhonikidze Institute in Moscow and in similar teaching institutions in Leningrad, Kharkov and Sverdlovsk.

Limited by foreign-exchange allocations, a few managers or trainees have attended courses abroad (senior Bulgarians, for example, at the London Institute of Marketing, and young Poles at the European Institute for Business Administration, Fontainebleau), and the International Labour Organisation— additionally to the centres in eastern Europe—has provided funds for management study abroad.

Labour

The communist parties of eastern Europe took power in

the name of the working class. The Constitution of the GDR declares that the Republic 'is the political organisation of the working people in town and countryside who are jointly implementing socialism under the leadership of the working class and its Marxist-Leninist Party.... All political power in the German Democratic Republic is exercised by the working people.' Despite such declarations—similar throughout east Europe—such power has rested uniquely in the hands of the Party; notions of a pluralistic society were being explored by the Czechoslovak Party on the eve of the Soviet invasion, but for the present, as for twenty years past, no autonomous organisation has any countervailing weight.

In the economic field, foci of dissent to government policy through shareholding in private corporations have definitively been eliminated, and—though discussed in Czechoslovakia at the height of the 1968 ferment of ideas—workers' equity participation in sizeable industrial enterprises is beyond realistic prospect, and farming and retail co-operatives and mutual credit unions are under government supervision. The tacit right of nomination to senior posts in all non-governmental organisations is exercised by municipal or district Party committees for small societies and local branches, and by regional and central committees for the more important.

Four options open to the wage-earner in the West to moderate the strength of an employer are of scant significance in east Europe. In the first place, the alternative to employment in state enterprises is confined to farming, remuneration in which—due to discriminatory price control over their products—is normally well below the industrial earnings level, and self-employment, restricted by licensing and taxation. In the countries where massive urban immigration underwrote post-war industrialisation, many workers retain links with villages, to which they can return when the differential shifts in favour of farming. Everywhere save in Czechoslovakia and the GDR, in which the migration is past history, a substantial intermediate occupation exists of 'peasant-workers' (in Hungary *kétlaki*, 'two-placers') who possess or share in

145

small land-holdings and divide their year between agriculture and wage employment.

Although the state is virtually the sole employer, movement between its units by those seeking better terms, is—as already noted—unrestricted. High labour turnover is a matter of serious concern to the central authorities and to enterprises: in Bulgaria, for example, the number of job-changers in industry in 1967 was equal to half the industrial work-force. Any period spent between jobs means serious income loss—trivial unemployment pay is allowed in the GDR, but none at all elsewhere.

A second option to the domestic omni-employer is migration abroad. So little has been allowed since the war that its effect on the home labour market is quite insignificant. To the expulsion of ethnic groups in the immediate aftermath of hostilities (page 22) may be added to the later emigration of Jews from Poland and Rumania to Israel and of Turks from Bulgaria to Turkey, but there is no equivalent to the seasonal or long-term movement of manpower from southern Europe (including Yugoslavia) to the industrial north and west of the Continent. A few Bulgarians have worked in Czechoslovakia and the USSR and some Hungarians in the GDR; the Rumanian government has declared itself firmly against any similar flow, however small. Official and commercial business and tourism—another eastern European country is a far more frequent holiday-place than Western (hard currency) areas—are the predominant reasons for movement between eastern states.

Trade unions

The two other instruments of countervailing strength in industrial relations are interrelated—the power of trade unions and the right to strike. As for other bodies, political supervision (save in Czechoslovakia during 1968 and early 1969) is exercised over elections to trade unions, which the Party regards as collaborators in the economic activity overseen by the central authorities. Again to cite the GDR

Constitution, the trade unions 'play a decisive part in the solution of the tasks arising in ... planning and managing the national economy and in shaping working and living conditions ... and co-operate in enterprises and institutions in the drafting of plans'. That Constitution (of 1968) makes no reference to a right to strike, which had figured in its predecessor of 1949 but which had been formally eliminated by the Labour Law of 1961. No east European legislation—nor even the Yugoslav Constitution—authorises strikes, which nevertheless occur sporadically, but without the judicial protection and strike-pay associated with industrial disputes in the West. It remains to be seen how the right to strike, written into the new statutes of the Czechoslovak trade union movement in March 1969, will be implemented.

For the past two decades trade unions have been uninfluential at the national level and weak in the work-place bargaining envisaged for them by the central authorities. Branches have been so long subordinated to the direction of their regional and central committees, which have urged the government's interest in compliance with economic directives, and hence in collaboration with management, that it will take favourable political conditions and the replacement of many local officials for them to be an effective offset to managerial authority. The disuse of the strike and other direct industrial action has weakened the militancy of union officials and their solidarity with their members, although the annual negotiation of a 'collective contract' has doubtless allowed the occasional resolution of conflict over shop-floor and fringe conditions in favour of the union.

The 'Action Programme' of the Czechoslovak Communist Party, issued in April 1968 when the drive for liberalisation was at its zenith, stated that 'the trade unions' principal function should become more and more the defence of the workers and their employment and conditions'. Nearly a year later, when that Programme was patently in jeopardy, the Chairman of the Central Trade Union Council told its

Congress that 'the basic attitude of the trade unions to the Party cannot immobilise their independent approach, restrict their views or push them back to a secondary position of mere executors of Party decisions'. That autonomous line remained after the change of Party Secretary in April, and an editorial in the Unions' newspaper on 5 May 1969 emphasised that 'trade-union policy cannot do without a certain spirit of opposition to economic and state bodies. . . . It is now realised in the overwhelming majority of factories that the main activity of trade unions consists in doing something other than what the managers are doing.'

Polish trade unions began a move towards independence of government, Party and management in 1956, but their statutes of 1958 were already back in a Soviet-type mould and, after his country had participated in the invasion of Czechoslovakia, the Chairman of the Trade Union Council declared to the Party Central Committee (in September 1968) that 'revisionism tries to transform the trade unions into bodies which make demands aiming to break the mutual dependence of living standards and production. The trade unions have rejected these revisionist tendencies.'

Hungarian trade unions, which failed to emerge as a political force in 1956, have a leadership compliant to the Party, but which insists—in the words of its Secretary-General addressing the Party Congress in December 1966, on the eve of the economic reform—that 'trade unions have the right to express their opinions on all questions, and to express dissent even on questions which belong to the manager's sphere of authority'. In Bulgaria and Rumania the trade unions have been brought into central decision-making on economic affairs—in the one by representation on the new Committee for Economic Co-ordination, and in the other by making the Chairman of the Trade Union Council a member of the Council of Ministers—and economic reform has begun to enhance their position in the factory.

The enterprise is, however, the scene of a more significant development, the institution of direct worker consultation as the authority of the individual manager is increased.

The Workers' Councils, partly inspired by the Yugoslav example, which were in the forefront of the Hungarian and Polish revolts of 1956 soon lost both their political and their industrial roles. In November 1957 workers' councils in Hungary were replaced by 'factory councils': run by the works committee of the trade union, they had in effect the consultative powers of the union in production and labour discipline, plus the right to allocate operatives' incentive funds. Those with over 300 workers in enterprises were abolished in June 1966 and eventually replaced by 'supervising commissions', of whose maximum membership of nine, up to three are staff (two nominated by the trade-union committee and one a white-collar employee other than the manager); the majority on a supervising commission are nominees of the Minister chosen from outside the enterprise. Its function is 'to prepare comprehensive reports on the functioning of the enterprise and then to make suggestions to the Minister'. Both large plants and those without a supervising commission continue, of course, to have trade-union committees which, since 1966, have the right to be consulted on the appointment of the enterprise director.

Polish workers' councils, which at their peak in December 1957 had been established in one out of every three enterprises, were co-opted in December 1958 on to 'workers' self-government conferences' in which they were equal partners with the trade-union committee and the Party factory organisation. Because, as just observed, the trade-union is dominated by the Party, the council representatives thenceforward were in a minority. The Party Congress of November 1968, reviewing the reform, made this subordination clear in a resolution which 'rejected the revisionist concepts which undermine the role of central economic planning to replace it by the free market. . . . Further improvements in planning and management . . . cannot be separated from the leading role of the Party and from the correct fulfilment of other functions . . . by the trade unions and primarily workers' self-government.'

The democratic impetus from workers came in 1968 in Czechoslovakia through the trade unions, and in June the government published the principles on which a 'Law on the Enterprise' would be established. It envisaged that an 'overwhelming majority' of boards of management would be elected by the staff of the enterprise; management, state agencies and banks would together take up about one-third of seats. Postponed by the invasion, the draft was altered in February 1969 to authorise 'enterprise councils', which would have one-third staff, one-third management and one-third government representation.

A national conference of delegates from such boards set up on 'an experimental basis' and of other preparatory committees, held in Pilsen in January 1969, resolved themselves into an unofficial 'co-ordinating group', but in March both the Chairman of the Federal Council of Ministers and the Deputy Chairman of the Czech Council declared that the government would oppose any horizontal or vertical organisation because they implied the formation of an alternative political structure. The bill was withdrawn after the change of Party Secretary in April and the experimental boards were gradually dissolved. The Chairman of the Council of Ministers in a speech of October denounced 'Šik's programme of disturbing enterprise administration by self-management'. The focus of worker organisation had by then shifted to horizontal organisations of enterprise trade-union committees. The most notable example came as a complaint against the manner in which the central trade-union office was allegedly ignoring 'demands and criticism', to support which the works committees of a score of large factories in Prague resolved in June 1969 to withhold the component of their membership due financing the central office, while continuing to pay that for their industrial union, the metal workers. Strikes have, however, been political in objective, from the general protest stoppage just after the invasion to single demonstrations (one in Prague, for example, in May 1969 against the use of a factory canteen for a meeting of the Czechoslovak-Soviet Friendship Society).

Though without overt political implications, new forms of worker participation have accompanied management reform elsewhere in east Europe. 'Production committees' emerged in Bulgaria in enterprises experimentally on the new economic mechanism in 1965 and were extended to all industrial units the following year. Transformed into 'economic committees' (up to 15 members according to volume of employment), they were accorded wider powers in 1969. Previously, the director had not necessarily participated—implying that its business did not invariably warrant his presence—but in 1969 he became an *ex officio* member; in the early version of the committee he could ignore its advice, but in the present form disagreements have to be referred to the supervising authority and the trade-union committee can in defined circumstances veto decisions in the field of labour relations or protection. By the new terms of reference the economic committee has to approve the organisational and production structure of the enterprise, the distribution of premia and all measures undertaken in conformity with the targets of the industrial association.

Boards of management were established in Rumanian enterprises under a law of April 1968. Only one member in five (in the smallest) and one in four (in the biggest) is directly elected by workers to the board, which comprises five to twenty-one members according to the size of the factory. The chairman of the trade-union committee and the enterprise manager are *ex officio* members and the remainder are nominated by the authority supervising the enterprise. By the end of 1968 there were 31,000 members of such boards of which 22,000 were nominated by superior organisations; the remaining 9000 were representatives of staff and chairmen of factory trade-union committees. They have no power over the distribution of remuneration, although they decide upon the elaboration and application of working norms, and seem mainly concerned with discussing the general policy and technical problems of the enterprises.

In the GDR the industrial association has a 'social council' on which trade unions—rather than directly elected staff—are represented; trade unions, too, are the formal representatives on the 'production committees' and 'permanent production councils' of enterprises.

In Albania, a trade-union committee is statutorily organised in each enterprise, but during 1968, as part of a Chinese-style drive to deinstitutionalise the country, a campaign was launched for 'working-class control'. Officially described as 'a permanent, constant method for exercising working-class control in conditions of the dictatorship of the proletariat', it would 'continue as long as there are manifestations which are bureaucratic and alien to socialist ideology'. The movement is seen by its Party sponsors as comprising, first, Party and state supervision over all economic and social activity; second, 'control from below upward'; and third, mutual influence among workers. There is nothing novel in the first, while the second, in practice, seems to be exercised only outside industry—by local investigations into the running of schools, kindergartens, hospitals and retail shops. An example of the third appears typical, in which a group of workers from the Enver Hoxha Engineering Plant proceeded 'to exercise working-class control over the Natural Sciences Faculty of Tirana University'.

Incentives

To supplement the inadequate initiative of the managerial staff, the Soviet 'innovators and rationalisers movement' was everywhere adopted; the practice encouraged manual and technical workers to criticise the actions of management in technical matters and organisation, to submit proposals for change and to put forward inventions and improvements. 'Rationalisers' whose projects were accepted were rewarded, normally in proportion to the economies effected by the application of their suggestion, while 'innovators' could make the same arrangement, or, more recently, patent their idea. A variety of other shop-floor incentives were introduced to parallel the standard wage-system, usually involving team effort in competition with other teams or other factories, under such titles as 'Socialist Emulation' or 'Socialist Brigades'. Matching more the early stages of the directive system than the reforms of today, they have by no means been displaced. Since there has been no reform in Albania, it is understandable that 26,000 rationalisation proposals were put forward in that country during 1968; the figure implied that a suggestion was made by about one worker in every ten. In Rumania in 1963—before reform—ideas were propounded by one worker in every seven, just over half the proposals being by operatives and the remainder by technical and managerial staff. In Hungary, nevertheless, the most advanced in reform, the 'Socialist Brigade Movement' numbered 1·1 million in 1969, or nearly one industrial worker in three. When he addressed a national conference of these 'brigades' in April 1969, the First Secretary of the Party observed that the previous practice had tried to take account of two interests, of society and of the individual, whereas the new mechanism embraced in addition a third, the interest of the group—of, or within, the factory. 'One of the objectives of the reform of economic management', he claimed, 'has been to increase the effect of both moral and material incentives.'

Non-wage incentives available for the staff of the enter-prise as a whole have been accorded more ideological priority than individual remuneration in money in the USSR: they accord with the collective view of a socialist community. Some such provisions by the Soviet-type enterprise are no more than would be found in most large factories anywhere in a developed country—a canteen, a club, sports facilities (through the trade union)—together with government ser-vices (apprentice-training, industrial health, etc.) which may conveniently be located on the plant. Factory ownership of workers' flats in eastern Europe is, however, rarer than in the USSR, where undertakings on dwelling construction are a prominent feature of the 'collective contract', and may absorb 40 per cent of the enterprise 'stimulation fund'—fed on the basis of profits earned. There is more such 'company housing' in Czechoslovakia and Poland than in Hungary, and government policy thereon has varied from time to time, but most accommodation put up by the former capitalist firms for their employees was, on nationalisation, usually handed over to the local municipality. With new authority to spend on projects of their choice, many enterprises under the reforms are anxious to attract workers, or to keep experienced staff, by the offer of dwellings: labour is scarce in the Czech Lands, the GDR and Hungary, while factories in Bulgaria, Poland, Rumania and Slovakia continue to recruit new workers from the countryside. Very inadequate government investment in dwellings—new construction or the repair of existing building—during the first two or three five-year plans has resulted in a severe housing shortage in industrial towns; evidence of the ravages of war a quarter-century ago may still be seen in the cities which were worst hit.

Only in Poland (as in Yugoslavia) have rents been increased, though a revision is under consideration in Czechoslovakia; generally they are too low to allocate the demand. In recent years a flat can be bought in a 'co-operative' block (constructed by a state building firm to the orders of the savings bank, the municipality or an enterprise, which then sells to individuals). If vacated, the flat must be sold back at the purchase price for reallocation by the co-operative to the next applicant, for the ideological fear of private capital gains still prevails. In Poland higher-income earners may not rent factory or municipal flats, and are required to purchase their accommodation.

Such co-operatives are part of government policy to encourage saving for large lump-sum purchases when supplies are restricted much below the demand at the fixed price. Thus it is common practice for the entire price of a motor car to be deposited when the purchaser inscribes himself on a waiting list (of up to three years); payment long before delivery is reversed only in relatively few hire-purchase arrangements (which, as already mentioned, were introduced in 1958–9).

Retail shortages of specific qualities or types of domestic products persist, and imports of consumers' goods are generally below the demand at the selling price. The restructuring of wages, which is coming gradually with the economic reforms, will not have its proper incentive effects until shopping is fully normal.

The establishment of basic wage-tariffs—classified by occupation and degree of skill therein and graduated by industry—has already been described (pages 83–4): reflecting the priorities of the early 'fifties, coal-mining and steel-smelting were accorded high rank in wage differentials, as they were in the allocation of investments. It has nevertheless proved easier to change the pattern of new capital formation than to reshape the structure of wages. Real wages can no longer actually be cut, as they were under the first round of medium-term plans. Even then, the bulk of decline of wages in less-favoured industries (e.g. textiles and food-processing) relative to those in the priority sectors, took place while the cost of living was rising sharply: money wages had rarely to be reduced. Governments in eastern Europe have never been as avowedly deflationary as the Soviet, but they attach great importance to retail price stability. If, therefore, wages in the hitherto disfavoured sectors or in new industries (e.g. electronics or synthetic fibres) are to show a relative rise, the process must be gradual. The same conclusion is indicated by the need to keep women in gainful employment: housewives were brought into the work-force in the 'fifties by the depression of the breadwinner's real wage.

Other aspects of the wage-system, also briefly mentioned (page 85), need overhaul. The margin between unskilled and skilled labour and between manual and technical staff has been excessively narrowed. The least-skilled grades became little applied, because, to effect any recruitment, even untrained, workers were put into a higher skill-grade; to keep an experienced worker or to augment his pay, management would reclassify him above his rating; and the ideology of proletarianism and of 'narrowing the differences between physical and mental work' endowed the reduction of differentials, at least in the early days, with moral and political purpose. Indeed, in 1966, when the Albanian government embraced certain Chinese ideas on this theme, managerial salaries were actually cut and two years later they and other 'intellectual workers' were required to spend 30 days a year on manual tasks.

These problems are compounded in the guided-market system by the shift of part of remuneration to shares in profit. Hungary began a wage-tariff reform in 1964, four years before the introduction of the new economic system, but Czechoslovakia began to make both changes simultaneously in 1967. The feelings engendered by a relative increase in wages for technical and administrative staff were strong enough in early 1968 for Novotný to seek to avoid displacement by Dubček as First Secretary of the Czechoslovak Communist Party by appeals to workers against the reformers.

In Hungary, the first distribution of the proceeds of the sharing-fund, in early 1969, led to considerable resentment among workers. The regulations allow payment of up to 80 per cent of the basic salaries of the manager and his close associates (at most a dozen, in even the biggest enterprise), 50 per cent of the technical and administrative pay-roll and 15 per cent of the operative and clerical wage-bill. Few factories earned enough to pay such maxima, and many managements effected the distribution by multiplying the aggregate pay of each group by these proportions: managers received sizeable sums whereas workers were generally disappointed with their first experience of the 'new mechanism'. Their concern was partly engendered by the new conspicuousness of the distribution for managerial bonuses, which previously had been paid monthly, and there was something of a psychological error in the manner whereby the change was made.

Czechoslovakia and Hungary are faced more squarely than the other countries of eastern Europe with the need to re-fashion their industrial relations, but whenever there is a trend towards enterprise autonomy, the staff knows that the managers can no longer refer their problems to an anonymous higher authority. Workers' councils would institutionalise the confrontation, but in their absence trade-unions may be re-vitalised, or resort had to the unofficial or spontaneous strike. Yugoslavia experienced a wave of labour unrest around 1958 when worker 'self-management' was more formal than real and domestic and foreign competition began to disturb the hitherto stable patterns of income between director and worker, between industries and between plants. But their expression in industrial action was not a display of political opposition: indeed, the Constitution of 1953 then in force provided a 'Council of Producers' elected by workers in a bicameral Assembly with a Federal Council, elected through territorial constituencies.

Future trends

The course of relations between management, workers and the central authorities depends so much on political and international events as to defy prediction. But it is relevant to any forecast to identify the positions on economic reform taken by the interest groups concerned, and the political strategy of introducing change.

The groups capable of influencing the form of managing the economy are, primarily, the national political leadership (the highest office-holders of government and party); secondly, those comprising the remainder of the central authorities (among which for this purpose are to be dis-tinguished the planning and control bodies, the industrial ministries and the financial agencies); thirdly, the senior staff of industrial associations and enterprises whose classic responsibility has been plan execution, and fourthly, two 'mass groupings', membership of which overlap where both exist—the trade unions and the workers' councils.

Pressure upon governments for economic reform has been exerted by academic economists and, at times, of political stress by students and journalists; peripheral influence has been exercised by farm, consumer and artisan co-operatives and even a union of private shopkeepers (already existing in Hungary). Local and regional interests, expressed through administrations and elective councils, have influenced the shape of change in Czechoslovakia (the federal constitution and division of authority between the Czech Lands and Slovakia at the end of 1968) and in Rumania (the merger of party and local authorities the previous year).

In the two countries where reform has been most radical, the key group interrelationships concerning economic devolution have been those between the two groups first listed; the mass groups supported decentralisation in Czechoslovakia but were neutral in Hungary while in both the academic economists made interventions which strongly pressed the Party towards reform.

The Czechoslovak trend virtually originated among academic economists, thanks to the forceful personality of Šik, then Director of the Institute of Economics of the Academy of Sciences, and to his membership of the Party Central Committee. They were able to secure consent for reform in circumstances of patent economic crisis, but had to implement it under continuing political centralism. That centralism required that the details of the reform be discussed primarily with officials of the Party, and the preparatory commissions thus preponderantly brought together academic economists and the central Party staff. The planning and control agencies were left aside—although the Research Institute of the State Planning Commission (in a manner shown also in Poland) pressed for reform against the policy of its parent body; it is significant that these agencies were curtailed at an early stage (in the division of the combined statistics and control body and the demotion of the Planning Commission to a Ministry, equal in power to other ministries and not, as before, supra-ministerial). The financial authorities —as in most countries of east Europe—were initially reluctant to support reform, but it was they who took over the caucus of the second group when the first—after August 1968—stopped its drive for economic change and the academic economists—primarily because of Šik's exile—lost influence. The Research Institute of the Ministry of Finance became a force for continued reform, partly because the serious problems of the Czechoslovak economy were essentially monetary (in inflation, the foreign balance and convertibility); it is notable that all the amendments to the reform since mid-1968 have been fiscal.

In Hungary, by contrast, it was the financial and the control authorities which took the initiative, led by Timár, then Minister of Finance (later Deputy Prime Minister) and Csikós-Nagy, Director of the Price Office (which, by taking over responsibility for material allocation, became the key agency in the administration of the 1968 reform). The National Planning Office does not seem initially to have been a protagonist of reform and lost some authority, but once the changes have been made, its Financial Division, headed by a former banker, Gadó, moved into the van. Academic economists—more or less equally weighted between verbal and mathematical (whereas the latter had preponderated in the corresponding Czechoslovak groups)—were early proponents. As soon as the government and Party accepted the need for change—and put a full Party Secretary, Nyers, in charge—a dozen committees effected collaboration between working officials, the Party staff and academics to elaborate details. It proved to the benefit of reform that many economists (a calling proportionately more widespread in Hungary than in any other nation) combined academic and government posts and that plan executants (managers of large plants and the like) were ready and capable to propose workable changes.

The prompt and thorough inclusion of all the central interest groups in the preparation of the Hungarian reform influenced also the strategy of change. Three policies could be chosen; one is that of Hungary (like the 1965 reform in Yugoslavia), in a single bound, making all changes together. Another is that of experiment, the cautious introduction of measures separated in time and not affecting all enterprises at once, as by Czechoslovakia in 1958, Poland in 1956 and 1966 and Rumania in 1969. Finally there is the deliberately piecemeal introduction of changes which characterised Czechoslovakia in 1967–8, the GDR in 1964–7 and Bulgaria in 1966–9.

But through whom and whichever way the reforms have emerged, the clear beneficiary everywhere has been the manager of the industrial plant. Increasingly a professional rather than a technician, it is he who has gained the most in personal authority. In a term applied to the American scene three decades ago, east Europe may be approaching a 'managerial revolution'; but the place of the worker waits on events.

Appendix

Central government authorities concerned with industrial planning and management, 1969

(1) Central authorities chiefly concerned with planning and control;
(2) Financial system (titles of banks are not translated; the functions are (a) state bank, (b) general investment bank, (c) industrial bank, (d) commercial bank, (e) agricultural bank, (f) foreign-trade bank, (g) savings bank, (h) state insurance corporation);
(3) Industrial ministries;
(4) Other economic ministries.

ALBANIA

(1) State Planning Commission
Ministry of Finance
Ministry of State Control
Committee for Labour and Prices
Directorate of Statistics
(2) (a) Banka e Shtetit
(g) Arkë e Kursimit
(h) Sigurim i Pasurisë
(3) Ministry of Industry and Mining
(4) Ministry of Construction
Ministry of Agriculture
Ministry of Trade
Ministry of Communications

BULGARIA

(1) Committee for Economic Co-ordination
State Planning Committee
Ministry of Finance
Committee for State Control
Ministry of Labour and Social Welfare
Ministry of Supplies and State Reserves
Committee for Science and Technical Progress
Department of People's Councils
Committee on Prices
Central Statistical Administration

(2) (a) Bulgarska Narodna Banka
   (c) Bulgarska Promishlena Banka
   (d), (e) Bulgarska Zemedelska i Turgovska Banka
   (f) Bulgarska Vnushno-Torgovska Banka; Morskata Turgovska
   Banka
   (g) Drzhavna Spestovna Kasa
   (h) Drzhaven Zastrakhevatelen Institut

(3) Ministry of Chemical and Metallurgical Industry
   Ministry of Power and Fuel
   Ministry of Engineering
   Ministry of Forestry and Timber Industry
   Ministry of Light Industry
   Ministry of Agriculture and Food Industry

(4) Ministry of Construction and Architecture
   Ministry of Domestic Trade
   Ministry of Foreign Trade
   Ministry of Transport
   Ministry of Communications

CZECHOSLOVAKIA (Federal government)*

(1) Economic Council
   Ministry of Planning
   Ministry of Finance
   Ministry of Labour and Social Welfare
   Board for Technology and Investment
   Board for Prices
   Commission for Statistics

(2) (a) Státní Banka Československá
   (d) Obchodní Banka
   (f) Živnostenská Banka
   (g) Státńi Spořitelna Banka
   (h) Československi Státní Pojištovna

(3) Board for Industry

(4) Board for Agriculture and Nutrition
   Ministry of Foreign Trade
   Board for Transport
   Board for Posts and Telecommunications

   * Under the unitary government superseded on 1st January, 1969,
there were the following industrial ministries: Chemical Industry,
Mines and Quarries, Heavy Industry, Forestry and Water Conserva-
tion, Consumers' Goods Industry, Food Industry.

(1) State Planning Commission
Ministry of Finance
Workers' and Farmers' Inspectorate
Department of State for Labour and Incomes
Ministry of Material Supplies
Ministry of Science and Technology
Ministry for the Guidance and Control of *Bezirk* and *Kreis* Councils
Government Commission for Prices
State Central Administration for Statistics

(2) (a) Staatsbank der DDR
    (b), (c), (d) Industrie- und Handelsbank der DDR; Bank für Handwerk und Gewerbe
    (d) Deutsche Handelsbank
    (e) Landwirtschaftsbank der DDR
    (f) Deutsche Aussenhandelsbank AG
    (g) Sparkasse; Postsparkasse; Reichsbahnsparkasse
    (h) Deutsche Auslands- und Rückversicherungs AG

(3) Ministry of Mining, Metallurgy and Potash
Ministry of Basic Industries
Ministry of Chemical Industry
Ministry of Mechanical and Vehicle Engineering
Ministry of Electrical Engineering and Electronics
Ministry of Heavy Engineering and Plant
Ministry of Light Industry
Ministry for District-administered Industry and Food Industry

(4) Ministry of Construction
Agricultural Council
Department of State for Geology
Ministry of Trade and Supply
Ministry of External Economy
Ministry of Transport
Ministry of Postal Services and Communications
Department of State for the Co-ordinated Utilisation of Electronic Data Processing

HUNGARY

(1) National Planning Office
Ministry of Finance
Central Committee for Popular Supervision
Ministry of Labour
Office of Prices and Materials
National Board for Technical Development
Central Statistical Office

(2) (a) Magyar Nemzeti Bank
    (b) Magyar Beruházási Bank
    (f) Magyar Külkereskedelmi Bank
    (g) Országos Takarékpénztár
    (h) Állami Biztositó
(3) Ministry of Metallurgy and Engineering
    Ministry of Heavy Industry
    Ministry of Light Industry
    Ministry of Agriculture and Food
(4) Ministry of Construction and Urban Development
    Ministry of Domestic Trade
    Ministry of Foreign Trade
    Ministry of Transport and Posts

POLAND

(1) State Planning Commission
    Ministry of Finance
    Committee for Labour and Wages
    Committee on Science and Technology
    Commission for Prices
    Chief Statistical Administration
(2) (a) Narodowy Bank Polski
    (b) Bank Inwestycyjny
    (d) Bank Handlowy
    (e) Bank Rolny
    (g) Powszechna Kasa Oszczędności
    (h) Państwowy Zaklad Ubezpieczeń
(3) Ministry of Mining and Power
    Ministry of Chemical Industry
    Ministry of Heavy Industry
    Ministry of Engineering
    Ministry of Forestry and Timber Industry
    Ministry of Light Industry
    Ministry of Food Industry and Agricultural Procurement
    Committee for Small Industry
(4) Ministry of Agriculture
    Ministry of Construction and Building Materials Industry
    Ministry of Domestic Trade
    Ministry of Foreign Trade
    Ministry of Transport
    Ministry of Shipping
    Ministry of Communications

164

(1) Economic Council
State Planning Committee
Ministry of Finance
Ministry of Labour
Council for Scientific Research
Committee for Problems of Local Economy and Administration
Committee for Prices
Central Statistical Board

(2) (a) Banca Naţională
(b) Banca de Investiţii
(e) Banca Agricolă
(f) Banca de Comert Exterior
(g) Casa de Economii şi Consemnaţiuni
(h) Administraţia Asigurărilor de Stat

(3) Ministry of Mining
Ministry of Metallurgical Industry
Ministry of Chemical Industry
Ministry of Oil
Ministry of Electric Power
Ministry of Engineering
Ministry of the Timber Industry
Ministry of Building Materials
Ministry of Light Industry
Ministry of Food Industry

(4) Ministry of Industrial Construction
Ministry of Agriculture
Ministry of Domestic Trade
Ministry of Foreign Trade
Ministry of Transport
Ministry of Posts and Telecommunications

TABLE I   Financial balance of the State in Poland

REVENUE	EXPENDITURE
I. Financial accumulation of enterprises	I. Current expenditure
II. Depreciation	1. Current budget expenditure
III. Revenue of state budget	(a) national economy
1. Income from national economy	(b) social and cultural services
2. Payment from social and cultural establishments	(c) social insurance
3. Taxes and charges paid by the private sector	(d) public administration and justice
4. Taxes and charges paid by population	(e) internal transfers
5. Miscellaneous revenue	(f) estimate of price and wage changes
6. Social insurance	(g) non-distributed expenditures
IV. Public services	(h) expenditure from budget surplus
1. Payments from the socialist sector	2. Appropriations for public services
2. Payments from the private sector	3. Factory funds and co-operative funds
3. Payments from population	4. Credits to private sector and to population
V. Revenue of financial institutions	(a) credits for working capital
VI. Increase of money issue and savings	(b) credit sales transactions
VII. Payment of credits by the private sector and population	II. Accumulation expenditure
VIII. Miscellaneous revenue	1. Investment appropriations
	(a) investments in socialist sector
	(b) credits for private sector and population
	2. Outlays on major repairs and other delays
	(a) major repairs
	(b) mining damages
	3. Increase in stocks
	(a) industry
	(b) market stocks
	(c) other stocks
	4. Expenditure of state farms for increase in stocks
	III. Other expenditure
	IV. Reserves
TOTAL REVENUE	**TOTAL EXPENDITURE**

166

TABLE II Financial Plan in Rumania

RESOURCES	USES

1. Accumulation (state sector)
  (a) profit
  (b) turnover tax
	1. Investment

	2. Increase in domestic inventories
2. Depreciation allowances (state sector)	3. Capital maintenance (state sector)
3. Co-operatives, retained profits (indivisible fund)	4. Increase in working capital (state sector)

4. Co-operatives, income tax
  (a) handicraft and consumer co-operatives
  (b) collective farms
	5. Other expenditures for the national economy
	  (a) planned losses
	  (b) foreign trade subsidies
	  (c) other expenditures

5. Receipts from
  (a) foreign trade
  (b) machine-tractor stations
  (c) other revenues
	6. Co-operatives' investment

	7. Increase in credits to co-operatives

6. Taxes and legal charges
  (a) wage tax
  (b) pension premia
  (c) agricultural tax
  (d) handicraft and liberal professions tax
  (e) local taxes and fees
  (f) taxes, fees, stamp duty
  (g) share of State Insurance revenues
	8. Increase in state reserves

	9. Current government expenditures
	  (a) education
	  (b) culture
	  (c) health
	  (d) other

	10. Defence
	11. State administration

7. Other resources
  (a) from the state budget
  (b) from the local budget
	12. Repayments of credits
	  (a) home credits
	  (b) foreign credits

8. Resources from bank credits	13. Increase in credits granted abroad
9. Consumer net savings	14. Other budgetary expenditures
10. State Social Insurance	
TOTAL RESOURCES	TOTAL USES

TABLE III Balance of income and expenditure of households and private farms in Poland (1965 Plan)

INCOME

1. Remuneration covered by wage-bill
2. Reserve of wage-bill for over-fulfilment of industrial production plan
3. Remuneration not covered by wage-bill
   (a) from 'Enterprise Fund'
   (b) other
4. Business trips allowance
5. Social benefits
6. Private income of households and farms from sale of agricultural produce
7. Income of private sector from sales of goods and services to socialised sector
8. Credits to households and private farms by state financial institutions
   (a) for working capital
   (b) for fixed investment
   (c) for instalment purchases
9. Claims for personal and property cover met by state insurance corporation
10. Income from sale of non-agricultural goods
11. Other incomes

TOTAL INCOME

Balance reserve (excess of expenditure and increase in cash holdings and of savings over income)

EXPENDITURE

1. Purchase of goods
2. Purchase of goods from off-plan supplies from industry
3. Purchase of services
4. Tax payments
   (a) personal income tax
   (b) land tax paid by private farmers
   (c) turnover and income tax paid by private sector of production
   (d) other taxes and legal charges
5. Repayment of credits
   (a) working capital
   (b) fixed investment
   (c) instalment purchases
6. Insurance premia on personal and property policies
7. Subscriptions to social organisations (Workers' Party, trade unions etc.)
8. Other expenditures

TOTAL EXPENDITURE

Increase in the volume of cash holdings and due to depositors in the Savings Bank

Total expenditure and increase in cash holdings

TABLE IV.   Departmental division of industrial ministries in
             Rumania (with effect from October 1969)

1. *Ministry of Metallurgical Industry* (example of decentralised type)

   Ministerial College (of which Minister is Chairman)
   Directorate-General: Supply and Marketing
   Directorates: Planning and Finance
                   Technology and Development
                   Production Supervision
                   Control
                   Employment and Training
                   Secretarial and Administration
   Offices: Special Works
                   Legal and Arbitration Affairs

2. *Ministry of Engineering* (example of centralised type with export-
   import rights)

   Ministerial College (of which Minister is Chairman)
   Directorates-General: Supply and Marketing
                   Import, Export and Foreign Relations
                   Heavy Machinery and Equipment
                   Electronics
                   Machinery and Series Products
                   Branch Development and Innovation
   Directorates: Planning and Cooperation
                   Plan, Finance and Prices
                   Management Training
                   Employment and Training
                   Special Works
                   Control
                   Secretarial and Maintenance
   Office: Legal and Arbitration Affairs

TABLE V. Official classification for enterprise accounting

Form of number-ing	BULGARIA 2-digit-serial	CZECHOSLOVAKIA Decimal	GDR Decimal	HUNGARY Decimal	POLAND Decimal
GROUP 0	Fixed assets	Fixed assets and investments	Fixed assets	Fixed assets	Fixed assets
1	c	Inventories	Working capital, in real form and investment	Raw and other materials	Financial resources and credit
2	Inventories of materials and uninstalled equipment	Discounts	Working capital in cash	Financial resources	Discounts
3	Costs of production	Costs and profit-sharing	Costs by item	Resources	Materials and commodities
4	Finished products (internal use), saleable products and sales	Gains from sales and (other income)	Discounts	Costs by item	Costs by item
5	Packaging		Credits and advances	Indirect costs	Costs of production
6	Cash resources	Funds, discounts of gross revenue and accounts outside the balance-sheet	Income from services	Output	Products
7	Discounts	c	c	Products and semi-manufactures	Sales
8	Fixed assets taken out of use	c	Debts	Sales and (other) income	Financial results
9	Losses of real assets		Funds, credit, profits and losses		Investment and capital repairs
10	Funds and reserves				
11	Grants and bank credit				
12	Anticipated income				
13d	Financial results and accounts outside the balance-sheet				

Form of numbering	RUMANIA 3-digit serial *a*	RUMANIA Decimal *b*	USSR 2-digit serial	YUGOSLAVIA Decimal
GROUP				
0	Fixed assets	Accounts outside the balance-sheet	Fixed assets	Fixed assets and capital consumption
1	Raw and other materials	Fixed assets	Inventories of materials and uninstalled equipment	Account of financing and discounting
2	Wages	Working capital in real form	Costs of production	Inventories in real form and stocks of tools
3	Costs of production	Financial resources	Finished output commodities and sales	Operational costs and personal incomes
4	Execution of planned costs of production	Discounts	Cash	Output
5	Products and commodities	Outlays	Discounts	Inventories of finished products
6	Costs outside production	Revenue	Fixed assets taken out of use	Sales
7	Delivered output, work performed and services	Funds, reserves, grants and results	Losses	Financial results
8	Sales	Current accounts and credit	Reserves and funds	
9	Discounts with third parties	Investment	Grants and bank credit	Resources of permanent means
10			Financial results and accounts outside the balance-sheet	
11	Discounts between enterprises and central administration within same ministry			
12	Discounts between enterprise and autonomously financed subsidiaries			
13	Payments to state budget			

a Until December 1968. *b* From January 1969. *c* Specified as open for further uses. *d* Other entries for Rumania until 1968: 14. Inventory revaluation; 15. Losses; 16. Funds; 17. Reserves; 18. State grants and increment in working capital; 19. Bank credit; 20. Finance and receipts for special purposes; 21. Anticipated income; 22. Financial results; 23. Capital repairs to fixed assets; 24. Capital investment; 25. Accounts outside the balance-sheet.
Note: Except where indicated by parentheses, translation is literal.

Bibliography

IN THIS selective list two or three books have been chosen from each country to furnish a survey both of the directive system as it previously operated and of the economic reforms at the latest available date. A standard compilation of legal texts relating to industrial management is added where possible. The bibliography in English is similarly confined to books, but includes some dealing with economic development rather than management. The broad objectives and origins of the two most advanced reforms are set out by R. Nyers, *Gazdaságpolitikank és a gazdasági mechanizmus reformja*, B. Csikós-Nagy, *Általános és szocialista árelmélet*, both Kossuth Könyvkiadó, Budapest, 1968, and O. Šik, *Economika a zájmy*, Svoboda, Prague, 1968, the second edition of a book, the revised first edition of which was published in English, O. Šik, *Plan and Market under Socialism*, International Arts and Sciences Press, White Plains, N.Y. 1967.

Albanian

I. Elezi, *Bazat e shtetit dhe të së drejtës së RPSH*, University of Tirana Press, Tirana, 1959; H. Papajorgji, E. Luçi, *Mbi disa probleme të përgëndrimit, specializimit dhe kooperimit në industri*, Shtepi botonjese Naim Frasheri, Tirana, 1968.

Bulgarian

S. Bonev, *Planirane i ikonomcheskie lostove*, Izdatelstvo na BKP, Sofia, 1968; P. Saptsarev, S. Kalinov, *Sebestoimost i rentabelnost v promishlenoto predpriyate*, Nauka i izkustvo, Sofia, 1969.

Czech

K. Kouba and others, *Úvahy o socialistické ekonomice*, Svoboda, Prague, 1968; A. Precioso (ed.), *Národrohospodářské plánování v ČSSR*, Nakladatelství politické literatury, Prague, 1963; O. Turek, *O plánu, trhu a hospodářské politice*, Svoboda, Prague, 1967.

German

K. Fischer, *Betriebsanalyse in der volkseigenen Industrie*, Verlag die Wirtschaft, Berlin, 1962; D. Hunstock, H. Keller, *Zur Kreditplanung im neuen ökonomischen System*, Verlag die Wirtschaft, Berlin, 1966; E. Langner, H. Goldschmidt, *Die Produktionsfondsabgabe*, Verlag die Wirtschaft, Berlin, 1966.

Hungarian

I. Meznerics, *Pénzügyi jog a szocialista gazdálkodás uj rendszerében*, Budapest, 1969; J. Wilcsek (ed.), *Ipargazdaságtan*, 2 vols., Budapest, 1964 and 1966; *Az új gazdasági mechanizmus jogszabályainak gyüjtménye*, 2 vols., Budapest, 1968; all published by Közgazdasági és Jogi Könyvkiadó.

Polish

Z. Keck, *Skorowidz przepisów prawnych ogłoszonych w Dzienniku Ustaw i Monitorze Polskim w latach 1918–39 oraz 1944–67*, Wydawnictwo Prawnicze, Warsaw, 1968; J. M. Montias, *Central Planning in Poland*, Yale University Press, New Haven & London, 1962; M. Pohorille (ed.), *Ekonomia polityczna socjalizmu*, PWE, Warsaw, 1968; A. Wakar (ed.), *Zarys teorii gospodarki socjalistycznej*, PWN, Warsaw, 1968.

Rumanian

Curs de planificarea economiei naționale a RPR, 2 vols., Editura Didactică și Pedagogică, Bucharest, 1963; *Organizarea activității de conducere a întreprinderilor*, Editura Academiei, Bucharest, 1968; V. Rausser, *Bazele planificării economiei naționale*, Editura Academiei, Bucharest, 1968.

English

B. A. Balassa, *The Hungarian Experience in Economic Planning*, Yale University Press, New Haven, 1959; A. A. Brown, E. Neuberger, *International Trade and Central*

Planning, University of California Press, 1968 (which contains the paper by Neuberger referred to on page 107); B. Csikós-Nagy, *Pricing in Hungary*, Occasional Paper 19, Institute of Economic Affairs, London, 1968; G. R. Feiwel, *The Economics of a Socialist Enterprise: a Case Study of the Polish Firm*, Praeger, New York and London, 1965, and *New Economic Patterns in Czechoslovakia*, same publishers, 1968; G. R. Feiwel (ed.), *New Currents in Soviet-type Economies*, International Textbook Company, Scranton (Pa.), 1968; I. Friss (ed.), *Reform of the Economic Mechanism in Hungary*, Akadémia Kiadó, Budapest, 1969; M. Gamarnikow, *Economic Reforms in Eastern Europe*, Wayne State University Press, Detroit (Mich.), 1968; G. Garvy, *Money, Banking and Credit in Eastern Europe*, Federal Reserve Bank of New York, New York, 1966; M. C. Kaser, *Comecon: Integration Problems of the Planned Economies*, 2nd ed., Oxford University Press, London, 1967; G. Kemény, *Economic Planning in Hungary, 1947-49*, Royal Institute for International Affairs, London, 1952; J. Kornai, *Overcentralization in Economic Administration: A Critical Analysis Based on Experience in Hungarian Light Industry*, (trans. J. Knapp), Clarendon Press, Oxford, 1959 (from which the quotation on pages 67-8 is taken); J. Kornai, *Mathematical Planning of Structural Decisions*, North Holland Publishing Co., Amsterdam, and Akademiakiado, Budapest, 1967; J. M. Michal, *Central Planning in Czechoslovakia*, Stanford University Press, Stanford (Calif.), 1960; J. M. Montias, *Economic Development in Communist Rumania*, M.I.T. Press, Cambridge (Mass.), 1967; F. L. Pryor, *The Communist Foreign Trade System*, M.I.T. Press, Cambridge (Mass.) and Allen and Unwin, London, 1963; F. L. Pryor, *Public Expenditures in Communist and Capitalist Nations*, Yale Economic Growth Centre, New Haven (Conn.), and Allen and Unwin, London, 1968; L. D. Schweng, *Economic Planning in Hungary since 1938*, Mid-European Studies Centre, New York, 1951; L. Sirc, *Economic Devolution in Eastern Europe*, Longmans, London, 1969; N. Spulber, *The Economics of Communist Eastern Europe*, M.I.T. Press,

Cambridge (Mass.), 1957; S. Wellisz, *The Economies of the Soviet Bloc*, McGraw Hill, New York and London, 1964; A. Zauberman, *Industrial Progress in Poland, Czechoslovakia and East Germany, 1937–1962*, Oxford University Press, London and New York, 1964; J. G. Zieliński, *On the Theory of Socialist Planning*, Oxford University Press, Ibadan and London, 1968.

The annual *Economic Survey of Europe* published by the United Nations Economic Commission for Europe, Geneva, systematically reports on institutional changes; that for 1968 included a comparative analysis of economic reform in eastern Europe. Norman J. G. Pounds, *Eastern Europe*, Longmans, London, 1969, surveys in great detail the geography of the area, including lengthy studies of industrial development in each of the countries.

The quotations on pages 75 and 133 are taken respectively from Frederic M. Scherer, *The Weapons Acquisition Process: Economic Incentives*, Graduate School of Business Administration, Harvard University, 1964, and Leland J. Gordon, *Economics for Consumers*, 2nd ed., American Book Co., New York, 1944.

Business periodicals

Each east European country has a trades union newspaper and (except in Albania) a weekly business journal dealing with domestic planning and management questions; the GDR in addition publishes a monthly for private industry (*Private Wirtschaft*). The main monthly periodical for economic planning is usually that of the Planning Office and the principal measures and official speeches affecting the economy are reported in the daily paper published by each communist party.

	Business weekly	Trade-union daily	Party daily	Planning-office monthly
Albania	—	*Puna* (a) (Labour)	*Zëri i popullit* (Voice of the People)	*Ekonomia popullore* (People's Economy)
Bulgaria	*Ikonomicheski zhivot* (Economic Life)	*Trud* (Labour)	*Rabotnichesko delo* (Workers' News)	*Planovo stopanstvo* (Planned economy)
Czecho-slovakia	*Hospodářské noviny* (Business news)	*Práce* (Labour)	*Rudé Právo* (Red Right)	*Plánované hospodářství* (Planned economy)
GDR	*Die Wirtschaft* (The Economy)	*Tribüne* (Tribune)	*Neues Deutschland* (New Germany)	*Wirtschafts-wissenschaft* (b) (Economics)
Hungary	*Figyeló* (Observer)	*Népszava* (People's Voice)	*Népszabadság* (People's Freedom)	*Közgazdasági szemle* (c) (Economic Review)
Poland	*Życie gospodarcze* (Economic Life)	*Glos pracy* (Voice of Labour)	*Tribuna ludu* (People's Tribune)	*Gospodarka planowa* (Planned economy)
Rumania	*Viața economică* (Economic Life)	*Munca* (Labour)	*Scînteia* (The Spark)	*Probleme economice* (c) (Economic Problems)

(a) Twice weekly
(b) Published by *Die Wirtschaft*, not an official organ of the Planning Office.
(c) Organ of the Institute of Economics.

Index

INDEX

RENAISSANCE
LITERARY THEORY
AND PRACTICE